parenting autism

Nurturing *and* celebrating your unique child

Sanjukta B. Mukherji
MOM AND BEHAVIOR ANALYST

FREILING
PUBLISHING

First Paperback Edition

Some names, businesses, places, events, locales, incidents, and identifying details inside this book have been changed to protect the privacy of individuals.

Published by Freiling Publishing, a division of Freiling Agency, LLC.

P.O. Box 1264
Warrenton, VA 20188

www.FreilingPublishing.com

ISBN: 978-1-956267-10-5

Printed in the United States of America

To my son, my sun.
To my daughter, my fulfillment.

table of contents

acknowledgments

I AM GRATEFUL to all the teachers, therapists, and various professionals who have played such an instrumental part in shaping our son to be what he is today. Your lessons and guidance have meant the world to us, and "thank you" is a very small measure of what we truly feel.

I have been blessed to learn from some of the best in the field. I am grateful to my mentors over the years—my professors, co-workers, and supervisors. Your support, encouragement, and belief made me feel that nothing was impossible.

To my wonderful family—my husband and children—thank you for having my back and helping me spread my wings. To my husband, thank you for the extraordinary dedication to the children, for reasoning through disagreements, for spurring me on and making sure I dream impossible dreams. To my daughter, thank you for the myriad joys of parenthood. We dream together, disagree, and then dream again!

I am indebted to my parents and to my soul, my sister, for being there as my pillars of strength throughout. You all encouraged, listened, supported, and inspired me to strive ahead, no matter what. What an extraordinary circle of love!

Thank you to caring and supportive grandparents/parents-in-law, sister-in-law/aunt for cheering on and celebrating every progress, and for relentlessly advocating for their grandson/ nephew.

Thank you also to my group of cheerleaders—my extended family and friends—for the laughs, chats, and fun times! You will never know how therapeutic and uplifting that has been.

To my students, from whom I have learned every day I am grateful that you taught me to look through your perspectives for a different way of understanding. You have helped me to find happiness and contentment in the smallest of things. I cannot thank you enough for all the moments of pure delight you have brought me.

Finally, to my brave son, who is the genesis of all things pure and noble. Thank you for lighting the path of unconditional love and boundless joys. Because of you, I am.

introduction

Why fit in when you were born to stand out?
—Dr. Seuss

THIS BOOK IS a culmination of approximately two decades of life and professional experiences of traversing a journey with a loved one diagnosed with Autism Spectrum Disorder (ASD). Professionally, the experiences have been varied, across a wide range of ages of learners, differing cognitive levels of functioning, and diverse settings of instructions. Through this continuing journey, I have had the great fortune of coming across many superheroes—caped or not—with extraordinary superpowers. They have learned diligently and slogged with utter dedication, with smiles on their faces and optimism defining their characters. They have never given up as they valiantly battled, squashed adversities and blazed ahead.

My son was diagnosed sixteen years back, when "autism" was not such a commonly heard-of condition. His diagnosis changed our lives in profound ways. The journey that seemed physically and emotionally challenging during the early days, seems a wondrous and remarkable voyage now! Our thoughts, understanding, and awareness regarding autism have been overhauled during these intervening years. The acceptance of "what-is" has given rise to the aspiration of "what-can-be"! I walk this path as a parent first and then as a professional. There is no doubt that my professional goals are intricately linked with the dreams and aspirations that I hold for my son. I have been able to stretch out my arms and open my heart, and now so many reside there—the superheroes with their superpowers!

This is not a book of how-tos; rather, it is sharing experiences and connecting them with available evidence-based strategies. The book has chapters that summarize key aspects as we navigate each area of interest. From assessment, early intervention, and special education nitty-gritties to being out and about in the community, the chapters attempt to provide some strategies that have worked for our family or my students over the years. Laced throughout the book are concepts based on the science of Behavior Analysis—not sitting at a desk and being bombarded with flashcards kind of suggestions, but living life and enjoying the moments kind of strategies. Applied Behavior Analysis (ABA) is an evidence-based intervention strategy, with many different teaching methodologies. Not all of these aspects may be suited for all learners, and that is well taken. Contrary to popular belief, the science of applied behavior analysis spans many fields, as is deemed befitting for the anticipated outcomes in each area. I have put forth strategies here that any child or student may benefit from—not just a child with special needs—if there is a perceived need. These strategies can be easily implemented across settings. The aim is to provide helpful tips and tricks that are practical and can be implemented effectively in any situation. The overarching intervention goals from my clinical perspective is to have a person-centered approach that is informed, and embody two simple values; being kind and compassionate.

The name "Rishi" is not my son's real name. His grandparents had suggested it at birth, and I thought it would be the perfect name to refer to him in the book. I did talk to my son about this project and explained what I was sharing. He smiled and said "yes"—rocked his body and clapped—a sign that he was excited with the prospect. All of the personal stories referred to in the book are from birth to ten years of age. Each chapter opens with our personal story from a parent's perspective and then goes into my experiences and takeaways from a professional perspective. I hope all caregivers, teachers, therapists, and professionals working in the field will find some beneficial information here.

I have referred to the pronoun "he" throughout the book as a general representative term, mainly for ease of reading and brevity. "He" is purported to be gender neutral, and it refers to all individuals with different abilities, and anyone who may benefit from these strategies. Please read it as such. Equally, the terms "special needs" or "special child" have been applied to denote an individual who has a formal diagnosis of any developmental and/or intellectual disability. Since my experiences are primarily in working with individuals diagnosed with ASD, I have considered autism as the primary diagnosis for the purposes of this book. The autism spectrum is vast, with people of different abilities and needs. The supports that they may require are varied as well. There is no one-size-fits-all intervention strategy here. While I have tried to provide strategies for various situations, please know that these are based on the general science of behavior analysis, for individuals who may benefit from the interventions suggested. Each child is different, the circumstances are unique. Please follow recommendations from your child's clinician/teachers for specifics.

Every day and in so many ways, my son embodies virtues that are all but lost in this world: a person bound by structures and routines in a disciplined way, content and happy with the smallest things of life, simple and pure emotions, hardworking, honest and true. He has no ill feelings toward others. He does not know what a "lie" is. He shows no pretences; he is All Real. How many of us can claim to possess even a fraction of these qualities? And how many of us with special children will put an instant stamp on their loved ones for possessing all of these attributes and more?

This journey has been as much of self realization while trying to parent or teach or train. I have realized that we often talk about our special children in front of them, assuming they have not heard or understood anything that we said. I would like to caution strongly against that. Similarly, as a parent I firmly believe that our stress rubs off on our children as well. They feel insecure if we are agitated and seemingly out of control in a tough situation. As best as possible, keeping a calm demeanor when things are rough will help our child breathe easier. Finally, keep the faith. I know how tough it can get and how insurmountable the challenge may seem at times, but it does get better. Hang in there—the hard work does pay off!

Here is an exercise for you. Pause your reading and search the phrase "Traits of autistic people" in your search bar and see what comes up. You will see page after page filled with "Autistic people cannot..." "Are not good with..." "Have difficulties with..." kind of statements. Before ANY positive attributes come up, you will see only deficits starting with "cannot." But we, as caregivers and professionals, know better, right? We know their capabilities, we know their potential, and we know their mettle.

With that, the ultimate goal of this book is threefold:

- Celebrating the uniqueness of our loved one exactly as God made them to be,
- Ensuring that we hear their voice and their choices in all that they do, and
- For our loved ones to enjoy a quality of life that is centered around their uniqueness and lived on their terms.

Thank you for reading!

~~~~~~~~~~~~~~~~

Piglet: How do you spell "Love"?

Pooh: You don't spell it. You feel it!

—Winnie the Pooh
~~~~~~~~~~~~~~~~

1

the beginnings

I have heard there are troubles
Of more than one kind.
Some come from ahead
And some come from behind.
But I've bought a big bat.
I'm all ready, you see.
Now my troubles are going
To have troubles with me!
—Dr. Seuss

Rishi's Story

"THE PRICE IS *Right!*"

Rishi whooshed down the hallway, his little feet carefully avoiding some stainless steel pan covers and Lego blocks scattered on the floor, as Bob Barker animatedly declared the tagline in his trademark tone on the television. He ran up to the screen, his hands trying to feel the giant spinning wheel, mesmerized with all the flashing lights and the ting-ting-ting chime, till it came to a stop on a number. And just like that, his engagement with the television was over, as if someone had just turned the switch off within him. He looked around listlessly and took off—back at his spot in the small walk-in closet at our apartment, busy spinning the wheel of the dumpster truck.

Rishi was all of 1.5 years old then. A sweet little adorable toddler—mostly fuss-free as long as he had what he loved, immersed in his own little world. I was a stay-at-home parent, new to the United States, trying to learn the ropes in this promised land, so different from the home I had known. As most immigrant families are familiar with, the leap in cultures and the way of living take some time to get used to. I would yearn to be in the midst of din and bustle, a "normal" state of affairs for me. Instead, the solitude made me homesick, and the silence rang in my ears. I would put the television on during the day for some noise, and I would pretend there were people with me. The adjustment was hard on me, and much harder on my baby, I mused. We all needed time to settle.

The loneliness seemed more acute since there seemed to be no special activities that Rishi and I did "together." The neighbors with children about his age would talk about the accomplishments of their respective children, while I would scan my brain to find similarities. I realized that Rishi never really engaged in any toddler shows in particular—something other parents were getting concerned about. He had, instead, picked up his own favorite and extremely odd TV routines that were strange and incomprehensible to me, but apparently of great delight to him: advertisements for incontinence, psoriasis, and odd geriatric medications; the opening melody of a cooking show; and Bob Barker and *The Price Is Right*. The daytime target audiences perhaps necessitated these advertisements from the sponsors—or maybe he saw elderly people and remembered his grandparents? I was not quite certain, but those flashes of moments were a complete joy to him.

The other strange interest of Rishi that I found absolutely flabbergasting was his innate obsession with doors. He adored them all—automatic sliding doors, push doors, elevator doors that would open with a ding, and regular doors at home. He would blindly run toward any exit point to continually open and shut them with tremendous force, regardless of where his fingers lay. At home, we installed guards on the doors so he couldn't slam them and get hurt. Wherever we took him, we would take turns supervising him by the door where he "played," trying to figure out what exactly he found so interesting in random doors and being a step ahead of him to keep him safe. His play had a unique pattern to it. He loved light-up and musical toys and would incessantly press on the buttons to see the lights and listen to the sounds. I cannot call it "music," as he was never patient enough to listen to it entirely. I remember we had gotten a $10 dumpster toy truck from Walmart that played a tune from a popular TV show. Rishi never watched that show, but he would press the button over and over again to keep listening to that loud and scratchy tune seemingly every second of every day, the same exact way. It eventually gave way, as expected. Much to my extreme irritation, we had to get him the exact same toy from Walmart again to keep him from falling apart and to maintain our sanity!

At home we were all worried, especially as we asked ourselves, "Why is Rishi not talking?" We were convinced he could hear, but we were at a loss to fathom as to why he wouldn't talk. My continual nagging worry, however, was not the lack of speech, but the odd behavior patterns that he exhibited. "Why does my kid behave this way?" I would wonder, but I never thought too deep into it, perhaps as a means to escape the looming worry. I knew something was bothering me, but I never could lay a finger on what it was. I always found some reason or the other as an explanation, telling myself it would get better, and willed myself to not ponder further.

I would pour my heart out to his pediatrician, who had been listening to my concerns for over a year. He suggested daycare, social interactions with other children of Rishi's age, and asked us to collect ourselves. "The transition had been quite significant," he had opined. "Give him time." We promptly followed through on the suggestions by enrolling Rishi in a daycare. The teacher was always in high praise of him for never bothering her and that he was always content with just a few toys. With mixed feelings, we continued with the daycare and evening playtime with other children, hoping that Rishi was just a late bloomer, and that he would start talking any day. Strangely, neither did I find nor did anyone utter the word "autism" to me through this grappling time. And I wandered around—worried, anxious, frustrated, and groping in the dark for answers to my increasing anxiety and confusion.

It was Halloween. The neighborhood moms and kids made plans, and of course we were eager to join in. Rishi used to run wildly out in the open—I never could control him by myself, and I needed my husband to be around. We contemplated on how best to go about the trick-or-treating business. Putting him in the stroller seemed to be prudent to keep the situation under control. Like many boys of Rishi's age, he would be Spiderman. He had no idea who Spiderman was, though. We tried telling him, but he did not care. We got ready and set for the big day—this was his first Halloween with a bunch of kids. We were excited and perhaps a tad apprehensive. We desperately wanted everything to be "normal," but somehow we were not very confident.

That actually turned out to be an evening I will never forget. From the moment we put the costume on and got him out with a crowd of laughing screaming kids, to stopping every few seconds for a candy at a stranger's door (again, much to my surprise, he could be least bothered about the candy)—it was just a train wreck. Rishi screamed, shouted, tried to yank himself off the stroller, flailed his arms, and dissolved to pieces. Both his dad and I did all we could to get him to enjoy collecting that Reese's Peanut Butter Cup or that Snickers that the other kids were grabbing and stuffing into their pails, but here was my boy dissolving in tears in that sea of excitement. What was inexplicable to us was earlier that month, we had gone on a road trip to Niagara Falls—a good eight-hour drive. Rishi was perfectly behaved, the trip thoroughly enjoyable with precious moments spent with his grandparents. Yet, three houses down from ours, on the same street, in a few seconds, he dissolved. We got back home, harried, frustrated, and utterly clueless; and then we tore into each other. We said harsh words—words we didn't mean, but I guess there was nothing much to do, either. None of this made any sense; we were just reacting to the deep frustration this experience had left us with.

It's strange how we remember odd events from decades ago—people's faces, what they said, and how they said it. At the back of our minds, these comments remain stuck, perhaps because they had touched some very sensitive areas. These comments are also our cues that someone was noticing something out of the ordinary. My husband often made a reference to Dustin Hoffman's character in the motion picture *Rain Man* with respect to our son. I know I had gotten upset with him with a distorted logic of causality when, in reality, his sharp mind had made some accurate connections that we were not ready to put in words. Or perhaps I never believed in the accuracy of it! I offered possible solutions to any worry that would creep in my head. I believed in some baseless theories and doubted myself. I also let myself slip into a passive mental state. When I look back now, I feel I was almost looking in at myself from the outside, not really "living" the life I was living.

The Early Signs: Nagging Doubts

The Beginnings—always a very good place to start! This is the time we start noticing those little traits that seem to set our child apart from his typically developing peers. It may be as young as a few months that people may start noticing something atypical and may comment as such, even if rather innocently. The worry then creeps in, as do a million questions. Why doesn't he smile at me? Why is he not playing and interacting with a "peek-a-boo"/"patty cakes" game? Why is he not responding to his name? Can he hear? We are observing, having doubts, and brushing them aside as delusions of an over-imaginative mind—only for those thoughts to creep back in again.

We really are at a much better place now, as far as awareness and quick diagnosis of the signs of autism are concerned, than we were twenty years ago. Pediatricians, daycare staff, and parents themselves are always watchful of the early signs of autism. However, this still remains a most common query of all parents: How do I know? Truly, the only thing to do when you are in doubt is to follow your instinct and talk to your health care provider. This seems such an obvious statement to make—but I know, as a parent, that this can be one of the hardest conversations to have, even with yourself.

My son demonstrated some classical signs of autism from just a few months of age. People would often comment, "Look at his personality—he's not one to offer smiles for free!" or "He is so selective with who he'd choose to look at," by the time he was about eight months old. I may not have thought much of it then, but the truth is that people noticed, and they spoke about it. To bring oneself to acknowledge feelings and then bring it up with the partner is a daunting effort. Making them see what you're seeing, coming to terms with something you're not yet ready to hear, and processing and acting on the information you now have are excruciatingly difficult and very heartbreaking. There may invariably be references of that family member who spoke late, or the dismissive "my-baby-does-that-too" kind of statements. For many, that conversation can spin off to a personal blame game, with far-reaching and sometimes life-changing consequences. However, this conversation cannot be put off, avoided, dismissed, or relegated to "another time." However difficult, the time is in the present, or rather as they say, get this done—yesterday!

Many children are indeed late bloomers. Just because a child does not talk, one may not assume autism. There are several factors that distinguish speech delay from autism, and I will try to list the main ones for easy reference. The first one is communication—no, not just the verbal kind. We are referring to the non-verbal reciprocal engagement kind of communication. Eye contact, a social smile on recognition of a familiar face, a connection with the caregiver, and give-and-take in a shared activity are all critical milestones in this domain. The baby should look in the direction of the speaker by orienting his face/body (and turning his head to look when slightly older); engaging with cause and effect toys appropriately; that is, a button is pressed and a music plays that they listen to and sway to the tune. These are the boxes you would need to be constantly checking. The child may still not verbalize words if there is a speech delay—but may well be engaging in these reciprocal communications as part of engagement and joint attention.

The second important aspect is understanding what is being said. So, with a speech delay, the child may not be able to express verbally, but he will be able to follow directions and understand what is being told to him. Simple instructions such as "Come here," "Sit down," "Stop," "Go," "Put in," etc., would be followed, whether in a game or with actual tasks. A child with suspected diagnosis of autism will have difficulty with this kind of receptive language. Even if he comprehends what is being said, he may exhibit difficulty carrying out the actions.

Many children advance appropriately on the development scale and then experience a sudden loss of language and reciprocity. This is a red flag that must be investigated at the earliest possible instance. The other signs of autism are familiar to many: resistance to change, repetitive behaviors, restricted interests, and exaggerated responses to sounds, smells, lights, textures, etc.

We must be vigilant and proactively consult with the healthcare provider should any of these areas be of concern.

Being Watchful, Perceptive and Aware

The American Association of Pediatrics (AAP) has recommended developmental testing for all children at their nine-month, eighteen-month, and thirty-month well check-ups. Specific screening for Autism Spectrum Disorders (ASD) is to be conducted at eighteen months and twenty-four months for all children during regular well check-ups. We are aware now that until eighteen months of age, a child on a typically developing growth path should be engaging with adults with socially appropriate eye contact and will imitate actions, point to things independently, show affection, hand something to you to play with, and say single words. Further information is available on the CDC website and others, but following are some of the critical areas:

- Between nine and fourteen months of age, a child must develop the skill of **pointing independently** with his index finger. Pointing independently indicates that the baby is developing crucial social and communication skills toward building relationships. It also establishes a moment of joint attention between the child and the caregiver, by the child not just gaining your attention but also attempting to elicit some reaction from you. If your child is taking your hand to point at something he needs, gently take his hand and guide it so that he is now pointing toward it himself, with your help. Acknowledge and highly praise his efforts. As he gets more comfortable, start fading the amount of physical guidance (the hand over hand guidance) you give him, and eventually he may start pointing himself. Why do I use the term "may"? It is because as a parent, I see my son is able to point with confidence and accuracy when his preferred items are presented in a smaller array and within a reasonable proximity. If these items are placed very far away, he may still not be able to point accurately. This is a goal in progress!

- **Eye contact** is another milestone area of development—the child is observing your expressions, imitating your actions, and developing his non-verbal communication repertoire. Hold up a preferred toy or other item to your own eye level so your child will look at you. In this context, I think it is important to train socially appropriate eye contact. What I mean by that is when we talk to people, we look at them not to the point of staring but making fleeting eye contact—enough to let them know we are engaged, but not long enough for it to be awkward. Many people feel uncomfortable looking directly in the eyes of other people. In fact, this is considered to be a sign of disrespect in some cultures. In those cases, orienting the body toward the speaker gives a message that the learner is engaged but not disrespectful. I mention this since eye contact is a skill that is trained with gusto during the early intervention stage. For months, we may try to train the learner to look directly in the eye, which might be a very difficult skill for him to perform. There is no one size that can fit all, and we must be very cognizant of these individual differences when making programming decisions, whether as a clinician or a parent.

- **Imitation Skills** is another pivotal area that babies develop by the time they are around eight months of age. This opens up further areas of learning across such domains as social interaction, communication, and actions (gross motor skills), to mention some. Throughout our lives, we learn by imitation: when we go into a new environment, we look around to see how others are behaving, how they are dressed, what their voice levels are, etc., and we adjust our actions suitably. A lot of play-based motor movement activities are available that target to increase the general imitative repertoire of a child. Nursery rhymes with actions, "peek-a-boo," "patty cake," etc., are activities that can make training of this skill fun and playful.
- By eighteen months of age, a child should have single words of commonly used items in his environment as part of his **verbal communication** repertoire. This is the most voiced concern from parents and the hardest

> one to accomplish in many cases. For a child who is not uttering any words yet, we may start with a contextual utterance such as "buh" for a ball or bubble and slowly shape it to the target word. This can take some time—so be patient and hang in there! You play, you say, you sing—even if your child does not appear to be following you or engaging with intent.

Many healthcare providers will refer a child for an assessment if major development goals are not reached as early as eighteen months of age. A screening tool (for example, MCHAT—Modified Checklist for Autism in Toddlers) may be used to determine if there are any developmental delays, but it is not conclusive evidence of a condition, and it cannot replace a formal diagnostic assessment. It is believed that by two years of age, the diagnosis can be quite reliable. There are various diagnostic assessment tools that may be implemented. Assessments for autism typically have wait times, so in the interim, it would be best to be aware of what some of the requirements may be from various sources:

- The health plan will require an assessment from a qualified professional. This is the biggest area of trip up during enrollment in a therapy program. Many times a screening tool or educational diagnosis is provided, and therapy providers will not accept either. A formal diagnosis from a psychiatrist/developmental pediatrician/psychologist meeting DSM-V criteria would be required as a formal diagnosis of Autism.

- Most likely your child will be referred to further services such as behavioral therapy, speech therapy, occupational therapy, or physical therapy if diagnosed with ASD. Your health plan coverage will determine the extent of services and co-pay components for each. Some states will fund these services through Medicaid as well. You can start budgeting for critical resources: time and money.
- In the days of social media, you can take full advantage of the same by joining groups and sharing your concerns with other parents. You will be amazed at the kind of resources you come across. Just be mindful that laws and rules may vary across states.
- If you are getting too stressed, take some time for your self care. Do whatever floats your boat, and know that you are not alone. Your child may have some learning differences, but you will address those needs.

You. Got. This!

~~~~~~~~~~~~~~~~
~~~~~~~~~~~~~~~~

AT A GLANCE:

- Be aware of developmental milestones
- Follow your instincts
- Communicate clearly and openly with experts
- Distinguish speech delay from autism
- Learn assessment/screening requirements

Life is a journey to be experienced,
not a problem to be solved!
—Winnie the Pooh

2

getting the diagnosis: handling the truth

You'll be on your way up!
You'll be seeing great sights!
You'll join the high fliers who soar to high heights.
—Dr. Seuss

Rishi's Story

SPRING SPRUNG ON us with all her beauty. The morning newspaper was a thing with us then. One of the prominent news features was on kids with something called "autism." My husband asked me to read it, and then he said, "What do you think?" Rishi's three-year well checkup was due soon, and this time I decided to go prepared. I would tell the doctor—no, I would *show* him the strange ways Rishi played with odd things. I carried the dumpster toy truck and the stainless steel pan covers for him to spin. I also brought his favorite toothpaste tube with a picture of a teddy bear that he carried around as if it were a stuffed toy and licked throughout the day, absolutely adamant to let go of it. I would tell the doctor that I had to keep that toothpaste tube under his pillow when he went to bed if I wanted him to sleep. I was ready and prepared. I needed answers.

True to my plan, I demonstrated Rishi's engagement with all the above activities to the pediatrician. He looked through everything quizzically and said, "Maybe it's nothing, but I think we should get him assessed for autism." I went home, and at the earliest opportunity, I searched "What is Autism?" on the internet. In the early 2000s, the search was not what we know today, but it was sufficient. To this day, I feel that sense of huge relief sweeping over me when I read about the signs of autism. It was that "yes, yes, yes" moment when I finally found the answer I had been seeking, a riddle I had been able to solve. My child was not a conundrum anymore! I was angry with myself for not looking sooner. I was eager to get the assessment done and get started on how best we could help him.

Since the initial diagnostic assessment was months away, and there was an impending relocation, we decided that I would take Rishi and spend some time with our family in India while my husband would take care of the relocation and get settled in the new place. I would join him in our new abode and get started with the assessment process there. I was excited about this move, since the internet revealed that I was moving to a place with a lot more services in the early intervention space. Everything seemed rather expensive though—these were pre-healthcare plan coverage times, and all therapies were to be paid out of pocket. We were still happy that a variety of choices in therapies existed!

Once in India, we decided to visit the family pediatrician, Dr. C. Within a few minutes of seeing Rishi, he said definitively and confidently, "Oh, yes, he is on the autism spectrum."

"But how do you say that, doctor? He has not even done anything!" I was very curious to know how he could be so sure in such a short time.

Dr. C replied, "That's exactly what! He didn't do anything. He is oblivious to my presence—in a new place, with a stranger, he saw through me. He made no attempt to look for you, his mommy, nor made any attempt to ask me who I was. You've answered your own question."

All true. Rishi was referred to a diagnostic psychologist to be assessed for autism. Four hours and hundreds of questions later, I saw the words "Autism Spectrum Disorder" on paper, written next to my son's name. I called my husband to update him, the busy traffic drowning my trembling voice, and confirmed the news. He consoled me, but perhaps he felt that the assessment in the U.S. might have an alternate outcome. On my ride home, alone in the car with my little one, I cried. I cried as if the world had crumbled into tiny shattered pieces and I was all alone, to pick those pieces up and put them together.

My husband, a brilliant student, had graduated from premier educational institutes in Asia. In my mind, I had dreamt of my son going to premier educational institutes of the world, beginning in the U.S. All those dreams lay mutilated beyond recognition. I looked at my little guy, enthralled with the traffic outside—watching the spinning wheels of the cars, buses, and two-wheelers on the road. He was happy and content with his life, impervious to the paper I had just been handed and what it meant for him. And seeing him like that, knowing he would not know nor care nor understand, broke my heart into a million more pieces.

I could not understand why I wasn't relieved anymore, as I was a month back. I kept wondering how all this could be happening to me. Everything seemed unfair, surreal, and untrue. My head was scrambling with incoherent thoughts. I felt anger toward some people and frustration toward some others. I hugged my son and nuzzled his head. He was not too thrilled; the sudden disruption in observing those spinning wheels annoyed him. He protested with a grunt and shrugged me away. I looked outside—the world went on with its busy day, every person rushing in a whirring tizzy, oblivious to my pain. My eyes welled, trying to fathom how to process all that I had heard, what to feel other than numbness, and from where to muster the strength to navigate this journey I never signed up for.

I pulled myself together as I neared home, determined to stay strong for others. I broke the news, gently but clearly, to the doting grandparents and aunts, who cried in shock and deep sorrow. They had a lot of questions—What is it? How can it be? There must be a mistake. Surely there are other reasons a child didn't talk—and then, inevitably: Why us? I gave them some reasoning, some words of strength, and dismissed some of their concerns almost because I didn't want to hear them out loud. Those concerns and worrisome thoughts had been buzzing in my head all evening, but I was determined to wall in my vulnerability. I tried to reason with a steady voice while quivering inside, desperately wanting to hold on to every comforting word I was saying to them, trying to believe them myself. There was no immediate solace for anybody, just a deep gashing wound that kept bleeding.

Starting Out

Getting a diagnosis for your loved one is possibly that moment of reckoning that hits the hardest. Often parents find themselves going through the five stages of grief: denial of the diagnosis; anger toward other members of family/fate; bargaining, often with God—"I would give up anything, please make him better"; depression while dealing with reality; and finally, acceptance of the situation. For each of us, the journey through these stages may look very similar or very different. These stages may not even appear in distinct order, but overall, from my conversations with many parents across many cultures that I have come across, most of us would have gone through these stages with varying degrees of intensity. Some of us have reached the acceptance stage and are able to feel peace within ourselves; some of us are still getting there.

With a very young child, the prognosis remains unclear, which makes it harder not only to determine any tangible outcomes, but also what expectations to set in the journey ahead. It is very important for parents to acknowledge their feelings and have a way to express them. Scream, cry, swear—or whatever you need to do—just let it out of your system. Take your time, be gentle with yourself, and take care of your mental health and overall physical well being. A parent needs a tremendous amount of support at this stage to face and tackle a voyage of unknowns, while being emotionally very vulnerable and grief stricken. A trusted friend or family member, or someone you know is already on that journey, will be a valuable support for you to share emotions and experiences. Every decision henceforth will shape the development and growth of the child in a very direct way, and that very thought is intimidating. Personally, we consider ourselves extremely fortunate that our families came together in abundant support and always focused on the big picture—what is best for our child/their grandchild/their nephew.

The feeling of denial may last for a long time in many families, with varying degrees within partners. The feeling that someone has made an error in judgment while assessing, or that a label has been put on my child by someone to make some quick bucks and I am being duped, can be very strong. In our case, I think there was an acceptance of what-is from my end a lot sooner than my husband. He had a much harder road to acceptance and closure from his end—of the dreams and aspirations he held for his son. He has eventually gotten there, but the journey in crossing the bridge and making peace has been his own. I think it is critical for each partner to have the space, time, and path toward peace and then a move to action. Our mental coping mechanisms need to find that groove to acknowledgment and acceptance. Every person deserves the time and patience to get where one needs to be—to dream a new dream and celebrate a new victory.

This is the time when we stumbled across a passage written by a special needs parent, and that helped us a great deal to come to terms with our situation. I will attempt to paraphrase it:

> You buy a ticket to Italy. You've heard of the enchanting locales, enthralling architecture, and the exotic culinary delights, and you cannot wait to soak in the experience. Your flight lands, you disembark and find yourself in … Sweden! "Hey, hey," you holler. "My ticket says Italy. I didn't buy one for Sweden!" you exclaim.
>
> "Sorry, but you're here now, and you cannot leave," they say.
>
> You are upset, and nothing makes sense—you wanted Italy, and you feel that's what you deserved. But then you start looking around. Sure, there's no Michelangelo, but there's Larsson; there's no Colosseum, but there's the Royal Palace. Tagliatelle and truffle oil are not available,

but hey, those Swedish meatballs, the salmon, not to mention the lingonberries—those are pretty darn good, too! You start loving the place, the people, and everything about it. Of course, there'll always be the sorrow of not getting to Italy, but there sure is a great deal of unbridled joy in getting to know Sweden.

This made a lot of sense, and it framed a new perspective in our thinking. Our thought process and approach to facing this challenge were further refined with sound advice from a renowned neuro-developmental pediatrician, Dr. G who shaped the early years of Rishi and us. He gave us three main mantras as we started this new journey:

1. Work on your goals; leave everything else to God.
2. Keep it simple.
3. "Normal" is a myth.

In hindsight, this approach helped us tremendously to shape the early intervention for our son. In recent times, a respected mentor offered some further thoughts to this reframing: instead of questioning, "Why is it happening TO me?" how about we questioned, "Why is it happening FOR me?" Now we've changed the perspective—we chose to shift from holding a "Why Me" mindset to seeking a design in the wisdom of the universe. Applying this concept we may ask ourselves, is this journey making me a better person? Check. Have I explored areas I would have never done otherwise? Check. Am I able to appreciate and count my blessings? Check. Am I getting that supreme privilege of raising a human being who is free of malice, jealousy, and falsities, and who is happy and content with the smallest joys of life? Check, check, and more!

So how do we get started after receiving a diagnosis? You know that you are the person best suited to help your child. and your child deserves the best help there is. You will have to get up, dust off, and get to work with a vengeance. Autism is a lifelong learning process for all involved; however, the early intervention years are significant as the building blocks on which later progress will be made. These years will ensure that the child will gain the critical skills toward self-management and coping and will lay the foundations of adaptive skills. Once these are in place, other skill acquisitions may develop at a steady rate and generalize and maintain over time.

A lot of families want to know how best to get started in terms of therapies and other services. In all their concerns, I hear a refrain that is very important to be clarified. So let's gather around for this part, shall we? I cannot say this louder or clearer: it is compellingly vital to keep in mind that autism is not a disease to be "cured"—rather, it is a condition that presents itself as a lifelong condition. Your child is perfect in every way, a wondrous creation of God! No one has the power to "fix" an already perfect blessing from the Almighty; you have endless love to shower and support your child in his own journey. You are celebrating your child just the way he is, only giving him some tools to cope and manage himself in this crazy world of ours. Being a special needs parent gives you an added superpower—a cape, if you will! From now on, you are his voice until he is expressing himself. If he is unable to express his thoughts verbally, no one should ever assume that he has nothing to say. No one should ever doubt that he is not learning if outcomes are not evident right then and there—he is taking all the learning in, at his own pace and in his own time.

Being in the Know

The very first step in this journey is to educate yourself about the diagnosis—what it means, what the research indicates, and what may be some of the best practices in terms of intervention options available. Some organizations provide a roadmap of what to do after getting a diagnosis that may be helpful. There are many parent support organizations that provide group training on a variety of relevant topics across age groups that can be very valuable resources. Topics include basics of therapy, state laws regarding special education in schools, and procedures you would need to be aware of. And from here on: welcome to the world of acronyms and abbreviations! Random letters will suddenly mean everything to you, and you will almost be conversing in codes!

You will come across a variety of support groups on various social media platforms. You may have to sift the grain from the chaff with many of these groups, but overall, scanning through discussions and noting parent feedback will give you a fair idea of what exists out there and how they stack up. It feels wonderful to be able to share a plethora of the daily adventures of the "ours" kind—the ones that only those who wear those special capes would know and fully relate to. It can be members of that elusive support system who are non-judgmental, ready to lend a hand, and open in their communications. There is an inherent trust in these communications and shared experiences between parents that can rarely be re-created with anyone else. The groups should be able to motivate and uplift you, forming a secure circle of trust and kinship and abstaining from bickering and name-calling that borders on propaganda.

You will come across a long list of available therapies on these groups, and the process to shortlist therapies is a rather overwhelming one. On the one hand may be miracle cures promising quick and amazing results; on the other are the evidence-based practices that have mixed reviews from parents and self advocates. Some of the ways that may help navigate this maze would be:

1. To conduct a thorough research on the literature available for that particular therapeutic intervention from reliable websites and trusted sources.

2. To seek word-of-mouth references from caregivers that may help alleviate some doubts.
3. Remember that any therapeutic approach that sounds like a too-good-to-be-true miracle treatment almost certainly is a red flag.

I have been offered all kinds of miracles to "cure" autism—Rishi eating live fish, taking detox baths, consuming absurd products and supplements, undergoing processes to remove minerals from blood, and trying alternate medicinal treatments, to name some. They all had stunning claims, promising to treat a laundry list of conditions in a magically unreal timeframe. To be honest, my vulnerable mind has stopped to consider a few of these at times, before I tore myself away, angered that my vulnerability is for frauds to take advantage of and make a quick buck on. The bottom line is: there is no magic pill and no miracle cure, as there is no "disease" to "cure" in the first place!

In terms of best practices as far as available therapy options are concerned, Applied Behavior Analysis (ABA) is widely considered to be one of the leading evidence-based approaches available. ABA is a behavior-based therapy that focuses on principles of reinforcement to strengthen behaviors—whether learning a new skill or engaging in appropriate behaviors. Communication skills, social skills, and behavioral skills are imparted via this learning modality, by using positive reinforcement (or reward) to occasion the learning. There are many intervention strategies that are based on principles of ABA and can be effective for learners as well. Salient among these are:

- **Verbal Behavior Approach:** This approach teaches the functional application of words as the child learns them. Several components of language acquisition such as requesting items, labeling names of items, and having a conversation (back and forth communication) are taught. Further, identifying the functions, features, and classes of items are taught. For example: What do you use to eat with? (spoon and fork); Show me the big red round object (points to a red ball); Show me the desserts (points to ice cream, cake, pudding, etc). The child uses his own motivation to communicate and potentially increases his repertoire.
- **Pivotal Response System:** Pivotal areas of a child's development are targeted instead of just one behavior in a play-based approach. For instance, motivation will be trained and strengthened using a child's interests in toys and/or activities. The child will be provided access to the toy or activity when he requests it. Through play-based activities, the therapist will facilitate further language development and impart social skills and occasion-appropriate play behaviors using the child's natural interest or motivation. So training in one pivotal area will have positive learning opportunities in several others through

engaging and fun activities for the child. Similarly, encouraging self-management, initiating social interactions, etc., are pivotal areas that will have long-lasting impacts in various other areas and aspects of learning. These broad areas are "pivotal" as they unlock learning in many other subsequent and interrelated areas.

- **Early Start Denver Model:** This is a play and relationship-building therapy approach using naturally occurring contingencies to build on language and social and cognitive skills. Parent involvement is a necessity, and intervention is play based. Sessions are conducted by therapists and parents and use playtime or a daily routine. This intervention is best suited for very young children, up to four years of age, and is often referred to as the "playschool model." In the core, the intervention strategy is the development of fun and positive rapport with the therapist (or caregiver) through engaging activities. Language development is facilitated on the foundation of a positive relationship development.
- **Floortime** and **RDI** (Relationship Development Intervention) are relationship and play-based approaches that are considered to be alternatives to ABA. Family involvement is key in these approaches. In Floortime, the therapist (or caregiver) gets on the floor with the child and takes an active part in his play. For example, if the child is spinning car wheels, the Floortime therapist

will first spin wheels and then roll the car appropriately. When the child imitates this action, they will slowly get into more complex play-based routines with the car (driving it around, parking it, racing with other cars, etc.). The therapist will ensure that the child's lead is followed while he aims to expand the child's "circle of communication." The RDI approach is also a relationship-building model involving caregivers. The concept of "Dynamic Intelligence" is stressed as a factor to improve quality of life for learners. Dynamic Intelligence refers to encouraging flexibility in thought process, coping with change, integrating information from various sources, and using the information in the process of learning.

Occupational Therapy (OT) and Speech Therapy (ST) services are recommended for a majority of children diagnosed with autism. Each of these therapies targets a very specific area of development for the child. OT provides skills in physical, motor, social, and cognitive levels that enable the individual to function more effectively in his daily life. Sensory integration and daily living tasks such as feeding, dressing, etc., are areas that occupational therapists address successfully with therapeutic strategies and interventions. Many OTs also offer equestrian therapy (horse riding), which has been highly effective for many children. ST is another widely recommended service that helps in communication and speech disorders such as articulation, stuttering, etc. Speech therapists work with a wide range of individuals in the spectrum and have goals aligned for each child's learning needs using a multitude of techniques implemented individually or in a group. These two services are commonly offered by many ABA clinics as well as in the schools, and they are coordinated with clinicians and teachers to co-implement many overlapping goals and targets. Engaging in sports and outdoor activities such as playing in a playground with jungle gym structures, and participating in age-appropriate sports opportunities including swimming, biking, walking, or running in a safe environment, are natural ways for the child to learn and grow. Martial arts, music, dance, and painting are some pursuits that have been extremely effective for many children as well.

This is by no means a complete list of available options, but it is rather a quick overview of some therapy and intervention options that you may consider. I do not personally endorse any one program over other, but since my expertise is in ABA, I will explore some components of it in the following chapters.

In the early intervention stage, you may commonly find your child's progress to be in spurts. Don't let your heart sink; talk to your therapist/clinician and make sure consistency is being maintained in all the settings the child is in. Also, keep in mind that throwing in the kitchen sink and then some will not accelerate the pace of learning; rather, it may prove to be quite detrimental to the child's overall development. Just like us, our children need time to de-stress and recharge, and they should get that time. Once you find your balance in terms of which therapies to start with and your time schedule, it is best to stick to it for a while to give your child and yourself time to settle. Any further additions should be incremental in nature, so you can clearly track and chart your child's progress. Early intervention is the most critical foundation for your child, and this time should be most wisely invested.

~~~~~~~~~~~~~~~~

AT A GLANCE:

- Accepting the diagnosis
- The five stages of grief: denial, anger, bargaining, depression, acceptance
- Each partner needs space and time to accept
- Autism is not a disease to be "cured"
- Brief snapshot of available therapy options

When life gets you down, you know what you gotta do?
Just keep swimming!
Finding Nemo
~~~~~~~~~~~~~~~~

3

let's get started: early intervention

Today you are you,

That is truer than true.

There is no one alive

That is you-er than you.

—Dr. Seuss

Rishi's Story

"YOU'RE RISHI'S MOM? He said 'Hi' to me today!"

"Guess what, Mama? He actually put one pea in his mouth without gagging at lunch!"

"We did it, Mom—he zipped up his jacket all by himself!"

"Rishi waited in line AND kept walking in the hallway—we are so proud of him!"

What a high we were on! Rishi had started early intervention at the local elementary school a year earlier. The child study team had come home to assess, which was a part of their intake procedure. Rishi had remained his usual self—not upset, not crying, but seemingly unaware of the presence of five strangers in the living room. While everyone talked with me in turn, the speech pathologist focused her attention solely on Rishi—talking to him, jumping, rolling on the floor, blowing bubbles—all to get him to say any part of the word "bubbles." Rishi occasionally popped the bubbles, but he made no effort to utter anything. Two hours and half a bottle of bubbles later, he gave her "buh"! The speech therapist squealed in delight, praised Rishi effusively and excitedly let me know that she couldn't wait to start working with him. For me, hearing that "buh" was like a miracle. "If only you knew how much more I look forward to Rishi learning from you," I mused. I was in love already!

We were getting started on a journey in which the smallest of skills needed to be trained and taught. The enormity of the task was just about starting to sink in, and so was the significance of the challenge. How easy it was for other kids to learn, and how deliberate the effort had to be from our side for our child to learn. Our primary focus, however, was to get our child to talk; we were concerned about little else. We wanted him to call us "Mom" and "Dad," to ask for things at the store or to watch TV, to ask to go outside, or to demand to eat a sugary junk. We just wanted to hear his voice!

In the meantime, odd behavior patterns had set in which ended up being a norm with us. We were aware of these oddities, but somehow we accepted these patterns as the status quo, having received a resistance at the first attempt to alter them.

Rishi would drink water using the tiny cap of the packaged water bottle. He did have sippy cups, but counting along as he drank water (25 capfuls at a time; 37 now) became a much more fun activity than a sippy cup. He was picky about food and ate in a really strange fashion. He had a green Elmo potty chair. He would bring it and *plonk* it in the middle of the living room, sit on it fully dressed, and then eat, while repeatedly slamming buttons of a light-up toy. He used the potty chair as a seat instead of a chair at the dining table, and he refused to sit and eat at the table. I remember we even had a set route when we pulled out of our complex. We would always make a right turn, no matter where we needed to go, and then make a U-turn to go in the desired direction, so we do not upset him. We knew these behavior patterns were bizarre, but we continued with them nevertheless, almost as if we were ordered to by an unseen force. We would brush off queries of "Why do you do that with him?" with "At least he is eating/drinking/going places with us."

I had pored over research on the best way forward, as far as education and therapy were concerned, following his diagnosis. There seemed to be overwhelming support for Applied Behavior Analysis (ABA) interventions in private clinics, with the next best option being focused early intervention programs in schools. We came to the conclusion that as long as we could be in a good school district, public schooling was a very viable option since structured teaching was being implemented for academics and social skills—two areas of high interest for us. The state we were in was considered to be on the higher end of the special education totem pole, and we decided to get set with public school for pre-K and supplement with private ABA, speech and occupational therapy for Rishi. As the years progressed, we added feeding therapy, adaptive soccer, recreational therapy, and swimming lessons. More sports got added in the later years, per his interest. In hindsight, each one of these therapies helped him tremendously, even though at that time we were not exactly sure how much it was helping, if at all. I perhaps became more aware of his gains when a lot of the footprints started being visible in the rearview mirror. I am extremely glad that we kept up with therapies, his dad driving long distances for a 30-minute class, come rain, shine, or snow. Also, I must mention that free time or downtime was critical for Rishi—he got easily overwhelmed with a tight routine. We continued home ABA sessions for about two years, beginning with ten hours per week and then tapering off to about seven hours per week after school. We again picked it up some years later as part of home intervention. Speech/OT/swimming classes were on Saturdays. Feeding therapy was for four months or so, on a weekday. When we had more time, we added adaptive soccer offered by the local YMCA. As Rishi grew up and services became less available for the grown child (as if they all are supposed to magically snap out of their autism when they get older!!), we added such programs as Best Buddies, Special Olympics, etc., that offered age-appropriate activities he had an interest in, and enjoyed with his friends.

As I write this, everything seems to have perfectly seamless decision points—coherent, logical, and uninterrupted. In reality, however, we were living through a lot of emotional turmoil. There were arguments, differences of opinion expressed vociferously, questions, doubts, and even denials. The recurring doubts were: the progress was not fast enough, we were not doing enough, and time was being wasted. This was like walking on a tightrope with eyes closed and no pole to help with the balance. In all of this, some of our decisions were deliberate, but many others we had just rolled into, dictated primarily by circumstances or availability of resources. But I think what pulled us through was an unequivocal spotlight that was our son. For his dad, getting Rishi all the help he could was paramount. If someone had said to bathe Rishi in moondust, I know for a fact that his dad would have found a way to get it done.

The early start pre-K program was staffed by some of the most wonderful teachers, paraprofessionals, and therapists. Our family shall remain ever grateful to this confluence of educators. Hereon started our journey into this world of autism as a family. This path is a difficult one to tread on, with no place for the faint of heart. The physical exhaustion was one thing, but the emotional roller coaster was a heck of a ride. We celebrated every little success, raring to go at the next target, yet we felt disheartened by lack of progress in some areas. Rishi's younger sister was born by then, and managing an infant with him seemed exhausting. My husband's work had become increasingly travel based, and many days the biggest achievement was that my hair was still intact at the end of the day.

Getting Started

I want to head straight to point here about the criticality of a sound early intervention program. In theory, early intervention can start as early as eighteen months of age, though in practice, twenty-four to thirty months is generally when a child may receive a diagnosis and a family will seek services. This is the age when the brain is still forming or is "plastic," and because of this plasticity, interventions may be efficacious and have longer term positive effects on symptoms and later skills, as several research studies have suggested.[1] The goal of any early intervention program should be in areas that a typically developing peer is progressing as well, such as communication; social and emotional skills; physical and thinking skills. All states have their own early intervention programs, and you may get in touch with the appropriate agency for assessment and other requisite services. In the earlier chapter, I have listed some therapeutic approaches available that may be the best fit for your child and family. In this chapter, I will attempt to provide a detailed insight to the ABA intervention approach, since that is the only evidence-based intervention available and also my area of training and expertise. I have structured the following section in a question and answer

(Q&A) format, as these are the most frequently asked questions to me.

What is ABA?

ABA is a behavioral intervention approach that may be applied in a wide range of fields—sports, marketing, mental health, forensics, gerontology, animal training, and organizational behavior, to name a few.[2] However, the most popular among all these fields is the application and usage in teaching individuals diagnosed with autism spectrum disorders. ABA is based on operant conditioning, which involves the use of reinforcements (or rewards) to strengthen behaviors—whether to learn a new skill or engage in appropriate social behaviors. The goal of ABA is to teach skills and modify challenging behaviors. This is done by identifying the function of behavior (why is the child doing what they are doing) and teaching appropriate replacement behaviors. For instance, if the child screams when he is hungry, through the process of reinforcement, an ABA therapist will teach the child to appropriately request food, thereby modifying a maladaptive behavior (screaming), identifying the function (accessing an item), and teaching the skill of appropriate communication ("I want to eat") by verbally requesting, signing, or using an assistive device to make the request (replacement behavior).

How Do They Teach at the Clinics/Centers?

There are many ways to teach, but the most common that you may have seen is the Discrete Trial Method (DTT). It is a very structured approach with trials conducted at the table, reinforcement provided for correct responses, and a method to correct errors and collect data right away. This method has, quite erroneously, become the face of ABA. Often many therapists are unaware of other methods that exist, as perhaps they have primarily been trained in DTT alone. Other teaching methods are Incidental Teaching (or Natural Environment Teaching), which is more child-led and play-based and very often a part of a child's intervention approach. Precision Teaching and Direct Instruction are also ABA-based approaches, often implemented in a group setting such as a classroom.

What Are the Steps Toward Commencing Therapy?

Typically, ABA services commence with an age-appropriate assessment conducted by a Board Certified Behavior Analyst (BCBA) to determine areas of strength and deficits when compared to a typically developing peer. An individualized plan consisting of goals and targets across domains including communication, social interaction, adaptive behavior, etc., would be formulated to best mitigate any deficits and build on strengths. ABA is considered to be a medical model; hence, the BCBA will determine the hours of clinical therapy that would be medically necessary following this assessment to master these identified goals.

Where Can ABA Therapy Take Place?

The setting for ABA services should ideally be based on the need identified during the assessment: in the clinic, at school, at home, or in the community. Community settings may include the shopping mall, grocery store, playground, library, movie theater, restaurant, or hair salon—there may be no bar to teaching and learning. The overarching goal of ABA is for the child to thrive and be successful in the least restrictive setting, for skills and adaptive behaviors to generalize and maintain across settings, with natural reinforcements.

How Many Hours of Therapy Are Needed? For How Long Is Therapy Required?

The hours of therapy needed would be determined by the results of the assessment and the medical necessity as ascertained by the supervising BCBA. Therapy can be recommended for forty hours per week as the maximum limit for some clients or ten hours per week for some others. It is my view that the child should be available for a block of hours per day for ABA therapy to be effective. It is important to note, though, that the goal of ABA is never to have children attending long hours of therapy for years on end. Even if full-time therapy (thirty hours or more per week) may be recommended initially, these hours would be reduced as the child progresses. Ideally, services should be titrated or tapered off instead of coming to an abrupt end.

Who Teaches at an ABA Clinic?

The clinical team in an ABA clinic consists of a Board Certified Behavior Analyst (BCBA) or a BCBA-D. These two levels are clinicians who have undergone master's or doctoral-level academic coursework and an extensive fieldwork training component, finally passing a board examination to be certified by the Behavior Analysts Certification Board (BACB). There are also therapists who work directly with the children, Registered Behavior Technicians (RBTs), who complete an extensive training program overseen by a BCBA or BCBA-D before passing an examination at the board level.

How Do You Choose a Service Provider?

This is a tricky part, isn't it? Bigger isn't always better; people who promise you the moon may actually disappoint in cosmic proportions! When you are scouting, some aspects that you may want to consider are:

1. How long is the agency operating?
2. What is the BCBA caseload? (If they are too stretched, the quality of services may be adversely impacted.)
3. How often may you communicate with your child's BCBA?
4. Is there direct communication between the clinical team and parents? Will I receive detailed information on my child's day?
5. Are they flexible with scheduling meetings?
6. What is the absence policy for clients? (You want them to say that attendance is a requirement; otherwise, fidelity of services would be adversely impacted.)
7. Will the emphasis and focus of each session be to teach my child the way he learns best?
8. Will my child's privacy and dignity be upheld stringently?
9. What is the training policy for staff and parents?
10. What is the procedure to address grievance?

Yes, ABA is data driven, and technicians do have to gather data of trials as they go along, but no, your child is not a data point. He is not an aberration in the graph to be "fixed"; he is a person with a thinking head and choices to make. Be sure to verify that they are taking their time to pair with your child and having fun in their sessions. Your child's likes and dislikes should be paramount, with a humane and compassionate approach to the session.

Ultimately, the success of an ABA program depends on consistent practices, both from clinical staff and parents. Staff members need to be consistently trained on best practices, to maintain healthy ratios, to have quality supervision, and to make decisions that are data driven. Equally, no ABA intervention can be fully successful without active involvement from parents as well—attending regular parent training sessions, maintaining consistent attendance of their child, and being involved in the parental goals planned for the child.

One of the most common queries from parents is: what do you do in therapy for so many hours every day? Many parents feel that they would like the therapy to be at home to "keep an eye" or "be around." I will attempt to provide a side-by-side snapshot of the therapy day at home and at a clinic for your understanding.

ESSENTIAL COMPONENTS OF THERAPY	AT HOME	IN CLINIC
Building Rapport with the child	Engage in fun, play-based activities to establish a therapist as a person your child will look forward to/want to be with.	Same as home. May take several sessions to establish initially. Should be built in the session when the child is already familiar with therapists.

ESSENTIAL COMPONENTS OF THERAPY	AT HOME	IN CLINIC
Teaching methods to address goals and targets	Through individual one-on-one sessions at the desk, play or natural environment based training. Breaks built in throughout the session.	Through individual one-on-one sessions at the desk, play or natural environment based training, group training with peer groups. Breaks built in throughout the session.
What goals may be addressed?	Communication goals, adaptive behavior goals, life skills, any challenges specifically relating to interaction with caregivers/siblings at home.	All goals of home plus social interaction goals with peer group, school readiness goals with peer group.
Available resources	Therapist may carry and/or use home resources.	Center resources on a wide variety of domains and activities, including motor movement activities and specific equipment to support sensory needs.
Community goals	May be addressed per the family's needs.	Depends. May not be addressed directly, but caregiver training may be provided to address challenges. Some clinics may offer these services directly as well.

ESSENTIAL COMPONENTS OF THERAPY	AT HOME	IN CLINIC
Points to keep in mind	Structured play is an essential and critical component of therapy. There must be goals targeted through play in a sustained manner. Be mindful of your presence—the child may react adversely if they constantly see you around. The therapist will address challenging behaviors. They are not your guests or babysitters. Let them work through with your child and resist offering help unless they have requested it. More than one therapist must visit for generalization of skills (but not a new therapist for every session). Use parent training sessions to clarify any and all doubts that you may have.	Use the parent training opportunities to address concerns with supervising clinicians. New goals can be added any time there is a need. Copy of behavior plan and related training need to be provided on an ongoing basis. Request feedback on the day if you are not getting one. Request observation sessions to see how the therapists work with your child. Structured play remains a critical component and peer interaction opportunities built in all day. More than one therapist may work in a day, but they should not be switching every hour. You are an equal part of the team—make sure your concerns are addressed.

While ABA has emerged as a foundational pillar for intervention for autistic children, my work with adult self advocates has opened my eyes to a controversial side of this intervention approach. Many adults view ABA as "harmful" and believe that children should not be subject to this kind of intense, structured therapy approach at all. I continue to research on this topic to better understand the areas of objection from autistic adults and gain insights. Overall, the concerns that arise are: ABA makes the autistic child indistinguishable from his peers; the therapists are strict taskmasters, continuous demands are placed with expectations of a robotic response, long hours of therapy recommended for very young children; focus on elimination of behaviors considered to be problematic: lack of eye contact, self stimulatory behaviors, and demands for compliance placed during a meltdown.

All of these are very valid concerns that many practitioners are mindful of, and ensure they work with a compassionate approach. I know questions have been raised in the past about a 2.5-year-old receiving 30 hours of services; looking directly in the eye to train eye contact has been in conflict with a cultural norm, and therapists have been reminded to never run acquisition targets (in other words, to try to teach) during a meltdown episode. I also know that frequent staff training is conducted to address these issues at clinics. I have had, and continue to have, several clients for whom I have never implemented DTT as a method of instruction, including very sparing DTT for my own son. He never did well in the DTT structure, while some other clients have been extremely successful with that approach. In all of this, some of us clinicians may say, "Not me; I don't practice any of these concerns," but I also feel even one other person practicing a measure that may negatively impact a child is one too many.

My personal view on this issue is evolving as I learn and research, but as of now it stands at this point: ABA is evidence based offering various strategies that may be used to teach skills in many different areas. I would consider each individual learner's interests and temperament to decide which array of intervention strategies would work best for him to learn without it being a boring robotic drill. I like to utilize every natural opportunity for the child to learn, and I abhor the idea of a child sitting at the table with flashcards, matching "apple" 50 times a day. I also greatly dislike training individual goals and targets (example: 50 nouns, 75 action words) without teaching the application of these goals and connecting the learning to real life. However, I do like the structure that ABA presents, so it is easier for the learners at a clinic, classroom, home, or community to acquire a skill and generalize that learning. I like that a clinician's decision making is data driven, so there are no ambiguities on progress and efficacy. I also like that intervention is person centered and addresses the needs of children and their families. I like that I am able to conduct training of staff and parents on a continual basis, so as not to miss any aspect of the home-work intervention. Maintain that the goal of ABA is to provide just the adequate level of support so that the individual is successful in his environment in his own unique way.

So how do you safeguard and make sure that your child is receiving quality ABA services? Overall, your child should be looking forward to going to the center or seeing his therapist at home. The therapists must be the most fun people to be around. A child-led therapy approach builds on the interest of the child that the adults follow and not the other way around. The therapy center should be building on the strengths of the child and build his motivation. There must be consistent progress with learning new skills. There also must be active training of functional communication as replacement to any challenging behaviors that may be dangerous to himself and others, such as aggression, self-injurious behaviors, elopement, etc. You must be able to see consistent progress with not just data, but also with skills generalizing across settings. You should be able to contact the supervising BCBA at any time and speak freely about your concerns. Finally, trust your instincts. I cannot define "gut feeling," but as parents, that antenna is high and active; and as parents of special needs kids, it may be several notches higher. Whenever you are in the slightest doubt, reach out and have a conversation.

Ultimately, it is important to be mindful of a goal out of any therapy that you may choose for your child. What do you want out of it? As a parent and professional, my goal for my child and students align: to celebrate my child's uniqueness while helping him live an independent life where I am redundant. He must not need me to fulfill his daily needs. He should be able to cope, self-manage, and lead a fulfilling life. These are overarching life goals, and they may be in progress for a number of years. Personally, I know we have not reached quite a few of these goals yet, but we start setting the stones to train Rishi: being able to adapt to changing situations, to sit at a place and engage with something, to tolerate non-preferred tasks, to participate in activities as a family, and to start demonstrating some emotional regulation in difficult times. A practical and pragmatic approach may help to focus on longer-term goals for your child and start working towards those with full intent.

~~~~~~~~~~~~~~~~

AT A GLANCE:

- Early Intervention is a foundational building block
- ABA is an evidence-based intervention strategy
- There are recent controversies surrounding the approach
- Safeguarding against low-quality programs is imperative
- Having clear goals and objectives will help in getting the most out of sessions

If you keep on believing,
the dreams that you wish will come true.
—Cinderella
~~~~~~~~~~~~~~~~

4

play time: make a play!

There are points to be scored.
There are games to be won.
And the magical things you can do with that ball
Will make you the winning-est winner of all.
—Dr. Seuss

Rishi's Story

THE MIRTH OF the giggles filled the house. The bubbles wafted through the space, swathed in rainbow hues in the bright beam of sunlight that found its way inside our living room. Rishi rushed in to poke at them with his little index finger outstretched, the expectant eyes waiting—and pop! My boy's face lit up every time the bubbles floated in, laughing in abandon every time he popped one. Every one of those times, our hearts brimmed, seeing his unadulterated joy at popping a bubble.

Such a simple activity, perhaps carried out as routine by many, was a critical one for us. Rishi's therapist suggested that we encourage activities that he liked and try to have him say what he wanted, whatever he could. He had recently started signing for "more" and attempting to speak ("bubba" for "bubbles"), and we were to immediately grant him the item he wanted, with a lot of praise. The lids of pots and pans that he constantly spun around on tiled surfaces were out of reach, and the doors that he loved to bang shut as play now had barriers on them so he could no longer slam them. Play was getting a lot more intentional—we were having to put some thought into what he would play with and why, unlike granting him whatever odd play patterns he fancied as we did earlier. Rishi loved toys that spun, had lights, or had a cause-and-effect action. We mostly gravitated toward the infant aisle in the toy stores and got him the baby toys, even though he should have outgrown them according to his chronological age. We still got him those, only now we were having him request—"spin," "ball," "red," "green," etc.—as he played and took turns with us.

This was a phase of discovery for us. We realized his hand-eye coordination was exemplary. We were determined to figure out what areas he would find interest in and to train him on them. He loved all forms of water play, so swimming was a viable option. He was always tall for his age and loved the outdoors; hence, we were always on the lookout for age-appropriate physical play activities for him. We also observed Rishi's visual perceptual skills—the ability to interpret what the eyes see. Lost me there? Autistic kids are supposed to take longer to process, right? Yes and no. Rishi's visual skills were and continue to be very strong, while auditory inputs in terms of a lot of spoken words at a time confuse him a lot. These visual perceptual skills were very evident in the way he solved puzzles, found patterns in window panes and lattices, and saw the world around him peeping through his fingers and through much water play.

I so wished Rishi could tell me all the wondrous sights he was discovering every moment and I could share those with you. But here is an incident I will never forget from when he was about four years old. He sauntered in the kitchen one night, holding a photo frame, and declared, "Pentagon." He was always spot-on with shapes, so it seemed odd to me that he would say "pentagon" for a rectangular frame.

I stopped whatever I was doing, sat down, and said, "This is a rectangle, my love."

"Pentagon," he insisted.

I took the frame from him, counted the sides aloud, and reiterated, "Rectangle."

Those big eyes had a quizzical look in the direct eye contact he gave me, asserted "pentagon," and held out his hand, almost in a resigned way—as if he had given up on my inability to understand "pentagon."

I looked at the frame one more time, concentrating on the picture it contained, to find anything alluding to a pentagon. As I turned it around, I stopped. The frame had a stand in the back, allowing it to be set on a table, and sure enough, that had five sides—a pentagon. I was stupefied! Imagine him coming to me stating "pentagon" and not "rectangle." The eyes seeing the unusual, the brain organizing that information, and him sharing it with me. Imagine how many things I have missed because he had not wanted to or been able to share, nor had I been around to observe.

Play It by the Ear!

Given Rishi's proclivity for being outdoors and to help control the on-the-go hyperactivity, we looked for adaptive sports for him to participate in. Swim classes for special needs kids were identified, which his dad tirelessly took him to, an eighty-mile drive for a forty-minute class. No complaints ever, as long as Rishi learned. Learn he did, in his own way—keeping his head above water (pun intended), but swimming smoothly. In the last five years, he has competed in the area meets of the local Special Olympics chapter, and he has won two golds, one bronze, and multiple ribbons for his efforts. Not to mention that he has acquired a critical life skill, all because of his dad's persistence and his own diligence. We started adaptive soccer at the local YMCA when he was eight or nine years of age. It was a beloved sport of his dad's, and he had an ardent wish that the son would love it, too. The son, however, didn't quite take a great liking to it, but he loved playing with the soccer ball in his own way. The coach was wonderful, and he let Rishi run around in the open field, while we looked forward to meeting with the other parents on a Friday evening, not having to stress about our son running around in an open space unsupervised.

Another outdoor activity we introduced early on was biking. Rishi learned with training wheels and quite literally enjoyed the ride. The beginnings were not all that smooth, though—his home therapist would run around with him in our front courtyard, as he wobbled around in the bike, letting out a scream in a terrified way as he veered off the pathway or perceived an obstacle in the form of a sundry item strewn across his path. One particular neighbor didn't take this too kindly and would bark from his window, "KEEP THAT KID QUIET!!!" However, on we went, for twenty minutes in the evenings during the summer holidays, and the kid learned—quiet or not! (The terrified screams actually did stop in a week's time.) Now, his biking partner is his dad, and the boys love a good ride on crisp mornings over the weekend or during holidays, mapping out their paths, taking selfies, and enjoying their time together.

They say inspiration comes from places you would least expect. The Christmas present in the form of a Wii game console proved to be just that inspirational miracle for our family. It opened a whole new world for Rishi, as he discovered the amazing sports resort bundle on Wii. The visuals were interesting, but simple. The auditory stimuli consisted of a music score with some exclamations thrown in—no jarring sounds or long verbiage. The games themselves were all sports based—simple and straightforward. The conditions were perfect, and Rishi lapped it up.

He reveled in every game available, particularly bowling with a hundred pins. Over time, we were only too happy to transition him to the real deal, with the regular ten pins. He loved it—an individual sport, his strength in outstanding hand-eye coordination aptly used as the pins scattered in the alley.

His strengths in gross motor skills and quick reflexes were maximized with basketball as well, introduced during adaptive physical education classes at school. At six feet three inches tall, his height is a huge plus for basketball, even though he did not, and still does not, own a single bone of competitiveness in his body. He participates in the Special Olympics basketball seasons, and no matter how many social stories we read, color-coded team jerseys we put on, or verbal reminders we shadowed him with—if a friend asked for the basketball, he would simply hand it over. Finally, the coaches found a way to solve this problem—they stationed him right next to the hoop, so all he had to do was dunk the ball in when he got it, which he did to the fullest accuracy and reliability.

All Play and No Work?

So what is "play"? Very simply, play is any activity that one engages in for enjoyment or recreation. Play is regarded to be of such benefit to the healthy growth of children that the United Nations has deemed it to be the birthright of all children. Fostering creativity, improving physical skills, and encouraging positive emotional, social, and cognitive skills can be successfully attained through play.

One concern that I hear very often from parents is: "I have no idea what kind of therapy this is; they just seem to be playing!"

To that, I say, "Oh, yes, I hope they are, and if they are not, I earnestly hope they soon will be!"

Before I go into further details on the topic, let me share a peek into some very basic skills that we can and do address through play. This is by no means an exhaustive list, but it will give you a fair idea: peer interactions, sibling interactions, turn taking, rule following, accepting win/loss outcomes, demonstrating good sportsmanship, decision making, planning, waiting for turn, sharing, giving up items, cooperation with others, visual perceptual skills, listener responding skills, gross motor skills, fine motor skills, inculcating team spirit, participating in competitive play, appropriate social interaction skills, communication, eye contact, accepting others' choices, self regulation, and natural environment training. And many of the broad domains will have several subdomains with a list of skills of their own. Not so much of a child's play, for sure!

From the very outset as an infant, a baby starts to make connections with the world around him through play. I had earlier referred to joint attention—creating that bond with the parents through shared activities. We engage in shared activities such as story time, tummy time, or mommy-and-me movement play sessions, all with the aim to reinforce learning in domains of cognition, physical dexterity, emotions, and social interactions through songs, physical movements, books, toys, etc. Typically developing children will go through various stages of play, starting with solitary play (playing by themselves); onlooker play (watching others, not quite joining in yet); then transition to parallel play (playing alongside others, being aware of own personal property); associative play (bringing in elements from onlooker and parallel plays, still being interested in seeing how others are playing); and finally, cooperative play (actively engaging with other kids).

With children diagnosed with autism, given the deficits observed in social interaction and communication domains, play skills become even more critically important and salient toward a healthy development. For our children, however, play often becomes a form or outlet of self-stimulatory behaviors—repetitive behaviors such as spinning wheels of a car instead of playing with it appropriately, fixating on objects such as a flicker of a light by repeatedly pressing switches, or perseverating on certain body movements such as rocking their bodies or flapping their arms. Left to themselves, they would be at it with no complaints; the simplest demand placed toward a redirection may evoke a meltdown. One thing is absolutely critical to keep in mind, though: the idea is not to change your child's natural interest. Children engage in self stimulatory behaviors because of the comfort in self-regulation it brings them—the enjoyment derived from that activity may not be replaced by any other activity at that time.

Our job is to introduce other fun elements of play as well, ideally mimicking the motion of the self-stimulatory behavior. We are saying, "Hey, I know rocking your body makes you feel great, but have you tried this swing? This is really cool and fun, too!"

In the above context, sensory play assumes a vital role in our children's lives, as many children with autism exhibit sensory processing challenges. Per research, the exploration of senses helps build and develop nerve connections in the brain. In case of children with autism, certain sensory needs may be more salient than others, some children may seek more sensory feedback, while some others may resist it. For instance, some children may resist touch, while others may seek it by touching different textures. Similarly, some children may seek to balance their vestibular system by repeatedly seeking movement-based activities such as swinging or spinning. Children with challenges in the proprioceptive system may seek pressure from tight hugs, squeezes, etc. These areas of need must be identified with the help of an occupational therapist, and functional and play-based activities may be optimally identified.

A well-structured, effective early intervention program should have robust child-led play sessions. This setting is optimal for the Natural Environment Training (NET) modality of instructions. Keep in mind that this is not a situation in which the child is left to his own devices and he plays on his own, unattended or unsupervised. A play session is typically very well structured, peppered with preferred and less preferred activities, to ensure we are teaching new skills with novel or new activities. It also keeps up the child's inherent motivation by presenting familiar, preferred activities. This technique in behavioral terms is called "pairing." Just as we pair ourselves as a reinforcing, fun person to be around, so the child will be motivated and look forward to being with us in the first place, in the same way that we pair items or activities. Say, for instance, your child loves all things *Frozen*. We would play with something neutral—for instance, blocks—before playing with *Frozen*-related toys. This pairing of a neutral toy typically may start with a few seconds before we build it up to longer durations of play.

This process can be implemented to introduce various new activities and toys—books, board games, puzzles, worksheets, drawing/painting, new equipment in the playground, etc. My child needed a structured pairing process to play appropriately in the playground. His great interest was the swing, and swing only. We have umpteen anecdotes of severe meltdowns just because he had to give up the swing, either because we had to go home or we wanted him to try another piece of equipment such as the slide. With the help of his teachers at school and the therapist at home, we first had him try the spinning structures, which gave him the same inputs as the swing, to perhaps regulate his vestibular system. Slides, zip lines, and other structures were introduced one at a time, so as to not overwhelm him. By then, he had discovered the joys of a lot of activities other than the swing (though swings remained his ultimate favorite), and he seemed far more willing to try out newer adventures in the playground. We would always allocate the maximum amount of time for the swings, but we knew he had fun trying out all of the structures in the playground.

There are some important things to keep in mind with pairing—we pair when the child is in a compliant temperament with someone he trusts and has a good rapport with. The access to the neutral or novel activity is short initially, but it is increased in short increments every few days. And finally, try to introduce novelties one at a time, so as not to overwhelm the child. I am deliberately leaving parameters of time and duration wide open as each child will have his own learning curve. You as the caregiver, teacher, or therapist would be the best judge whether it is going to be thirty seconds or three minutes. Often, we are able to decide after what can be best described as trial and errors: the extent to which novel play remains an encouragement and not aversive or intrusive. We have to be cautious that we let our children explore their interests naturally and not because we said so.

Play It Up!

Learning to play appropriately by oneself or with friends is a skill that seems very innate but can be the hardest to train. From around three years of age, children begin demonstrating social or cooperative play, where they engage with others and items/activities to play in a meaningful manner. We start seeing the emergence of role playing, pretend playing, and making rules and following them—a give-and-take or cooperative approach with each other while they engage in a shared activity. Our kids have specific interests that may not overlap with anyone else's. Someone can tell you every last detail of the latest model of the floor scrubber, someone else is engulfed in the world of anime, yet another will flick a pencil in front of his eyes, while the fourth would give up anything to smell freshly laundered clothes.

One way to approach this would be for the trainers to participate in the same activity that the child is engaging in and then start to slowly shape the response. For instance, you spin the car wheel with your child and then introduce how the car rolls. Keeping the activity and interaction highly motivating will help in sustaining the interest and engagement from your child. The car rolls, but does it honk? Would the headlights light up or the doors open? Get some of the cool features and show him how they work. Show him how much you enjoy playing! He may not engage right away, but he will be more curious to explore beyond the wheels.

I recall how my son would be fixated on a toy laptop and would keep pressing one button repeatedly. He would scream and protest when I attempted to show him other buttons and what they did. I often thought he never saw or heard anything I showed. But several hours later, I would find him exploring the laptop—he would still go back to his favorite button, but only after checking out the toy a bit more.

It is very beneficial to have some goals for a play session if it is in the home environment. What do you want to achieve out of this? Are you training a pre-academic skill? Are you training him in turn taking and sharing with a sibling or yourself? Maybe you are helping him to follow the rules of a game and to be a good sport even when the outcome is unfavorable. It is important for us to be aware of what we want to achieve from that play session like any other therapy session.

Appropriate communication in various stages of verbal abilities can be trained. Requesting someone to come and play, scanning an array to look for a missing item such as a puzzle piece, or identifying objects, shapes, and colors are all examples of a wide variety of skills targeted in a play session. Many children may benefit from a visual support such as a script to occasion appropriate social communicative exchange while playing a game. My child needed a visual reminder to try different structures in the playground. Initially, we incorporated duration of engagement for each of the activities as well, but as his natural interest grew, we faded these supports off. Even now, he may seem completely disinterested in a group activity his peers are engaged in, but when given a choice to stay or leave, he would always choose to stay. He would engage in the activities with reminders, but he would stay on until the entire event had concluded and all his peers had left.

As the child gets older, supplementing therapies in controlled settings such as a school or clinic with engagement in sports and other creative pursuits such as dance, gymnastics, painting, music, etc., helps a great deal in generalization of acquired skills. The child has to follow instructions in a group from different people and exhibit some level of proficiency. These are vital skill sets in a child's learning curve, and they should be a part of their routine as much as possible.

For our family, Rishi's interests in activities such as bowling, biking, and swimming have served a greater purpose than skills to be checked off on paper. One of the mental agonies his dad faced while coming to terms with Rishi's diagnosis was the loss of quality "man time." He rued the loss of conversations, discussions, and arguments around sports, being an avid sports buff himself. It hurt him that they would not go to a ball game and talk about the game in progress, discuss the outcome, or review the players' performances. Yes, they cannot, since we are not in "Italy." But look, we are in "Sweden" now, and here is how they go for the "boys only" activities: an evening at the bowling alley; a swim in the pool followed by some Jacuzzi time; rollicking time swimming in the ocean; and exploring different trails in the neighborhood on their bikes. These moments are priceless, cherished, and the most precious in their own unique way.

~~~~~~~~~~~~~~~~
~~~~~~~~~~~~~~~~

AT A GLANCE:

- Play is a critical developmental skill
- Communication, social Interactions, and behavior domains and subdomains are addressed through play
- Pairing process to build rapport with child
- Pairing process to introduce variety in play
- Have goals based on natural interests

Don't just fly, SOAR!

—Dumbo the Elephant

5

behave! behavior modification and then some

Always remember

You are braver than you believe,

Stronger than you seem,

Smarter than you think and

Twice as beautiful

As you've ever imagined.

—Dr. Seuss

Rishi's Story

THE CLOUDS DRIFTED in the clear blue sky, carefree, toward their unknown destination. The resolute afternoon sun made its presence felt even in the caressing breeze. The pool water hummed its song and danced gleefully in a silvery shimmering delight. And shooting through the serene quietude of it all went a piercing "AAAAAHHHHHH!!"

R-e-w-i-n-d. The apartment was a gated community. The school bus picked up and dropped kids off outside the gate at designated times. The nightmare of our morning rush was amply compensated by the peaceful afternoon walk through the scenic complex grounds. The younger one was three by now and accompanied me every day to pick her brother up. Our typical routine was to stop by at the mailbox and wait at the picnic spot until the bus showed up. Our walk back was always through the pool area with Rishi. This day, we were rushed. We did not have the time to stop by the mailbox, so I decided we would do so on our way back. Instead of our regular path home, we set off toward the mailbox, stopping to exchange a few casual pleasantries with a neighbor on the way. The outcome of deviating from the usual routine was as above.

From infancy, Rishi seemed extremely fussy at times and impossibly content at others. The smallest things seemed to be highly upsetting to him: crowded places, unfamiliar people, a change in his routine, a new food item, sudden loud noises, and having to wait in general. Some of this was typical of children his age, but our friends could talk to their children and make them understand. My son cried and literally fell apart. There was no talking, no reasoning at that time. There was that moment of our child lying on the floor, crying, and us helpless, frustrated, angry, and completely clueless.

Rishi also showed no interest in making friends or playing with other children his age. For the most part, he seemed completely unaware of their presence around him. I remember him playing with the mulch at the play area or flicking pool water while other kids laughed and played together. As such, even he and his sister barely played together. Play time with his sibling was more like taking turns with reminders during an activity of interest such as a swing, merry-go-round, trampoline, or sensory play. It was hard to tell if he ever enjoyed company, as the conventional social signs—a smile, a spontaneous hug, asking for more play time, refusing to leave—seemed to be absent. Happiness was revealed in self-stimulatory behaviors such as rocking, jumping, or making noises. Refusal was displayed by a tantrum, crying, or screaming while laid out on the ground, wherever we might be. We were not sure how to interpret all of this—should we ask him to stop a repetitive behavior when we clearly could see he was happy? Should we not let him express his happiness however he wanted, even if it seemed out of the ordinary? How could he tell us appropriately that he was upset instead of the tantrums?

The Whats and the Whys

Applied Behavior Analysis (ABA) is a behavioral therapy intervention approach, and modification of behavior is one the main pillars of ABA. In essence, ABA deals with modification of behaviors of social significance, that is, intervention is planned only those behaviors that may be barriers to learning or leading a fulfilling life. These behaviors are identified by the individual themselves, or their immediate caregivers who have firsthand knowledge. Nobody has the power to alter who your child is, nor does anyone have the right to determine what should work for you or your child without consulting you. Behavior modification in its truest form is to impart tools of self-regulation for the indivual to function in the best possible way in his own environment. Hence, behavior goals must be established in consultation with the individual and if that is not possible, with you, the caregiver, regarding your concerns for your child. In the case of individuals who are able to advocate for themselves, listen to their concerns and difficulties and then work out a plan. It is a collaborative process, individualized to the needs and requirements that matter to each set of individuals in their own unique settings.

Further, the most important thing to keep in mind is that all behaviors of concern are essentially just a mode of communication. Your child is communicating his feelings, and we will have to shape that communication in a way that is easily understood by all. To achieve this goal, the ABA approach attempts to study the behavior of concern from various angles. The very first step is to examine the "what" of the behavior of concern—what is occurring, in what circumstances, and how are we reacting to it. This is referred to the ABCs of behavior:

A: **Antecedent**- What occurred PRIOR to the behavior of concern.

B: **Behavior**—Describing the behavior that is occurring in the PRESENT.

C: Consequence—What occurred AFTER that behavior (B) took place.

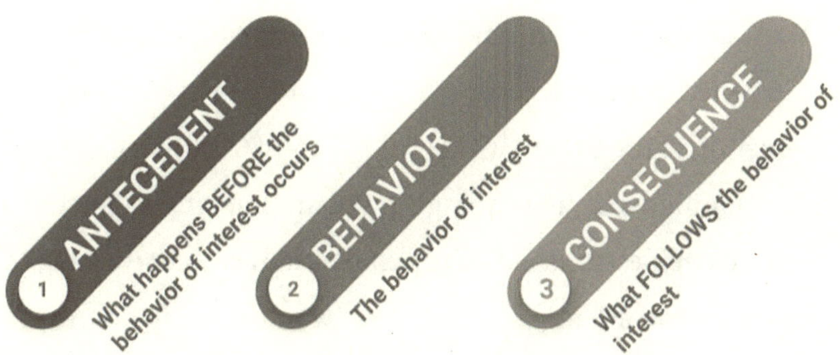

Very simply, the Antecedent (A) stage looks for the triggers. If your child has a hard time (say, a tantrum) at the store, you would examine what is happening at that time. You do not try to change anything at this point. You are just trying to objectively note the trigger systematically. What is happening when you go to the store? What is your child doing at this time? Are you in a particular area at the store?

Then you note the Behaviors (B). What does the tantrum look like? If you were an outsider looking in, what would you see? Again, you are objectively noting that down.

Finally, the Consequence (C). What did you do to get him to stop? Did you leave the store? Did you buy him something he loves such as candy or ice cream?

When you objectively note this down for all behaviors of concern, you will start seeing an emerging pattern. It could be a pattern of triggers in the form of a non-preferred demand placed, maybe to give up some item or activity and transition to something else, or perhaps you denied a request to access an item or activity. This emerging pattern is critically important for us to get to the following very crucial aspect—the whys of behavior.

In behavior analytic terms, the "why" of the behavior is known as Function of the Behavior—why is the child (or anyone, for that matter) doing what he is doing? There are four main functions that have been established as per empirical research: wanting to gain someone's attention; wanting to avoid or escape non-preferred tasks; wanting to access a preferred item or activity; and finally, sensory stimulation—bright lights, loud sudden noise, too many people, etc.

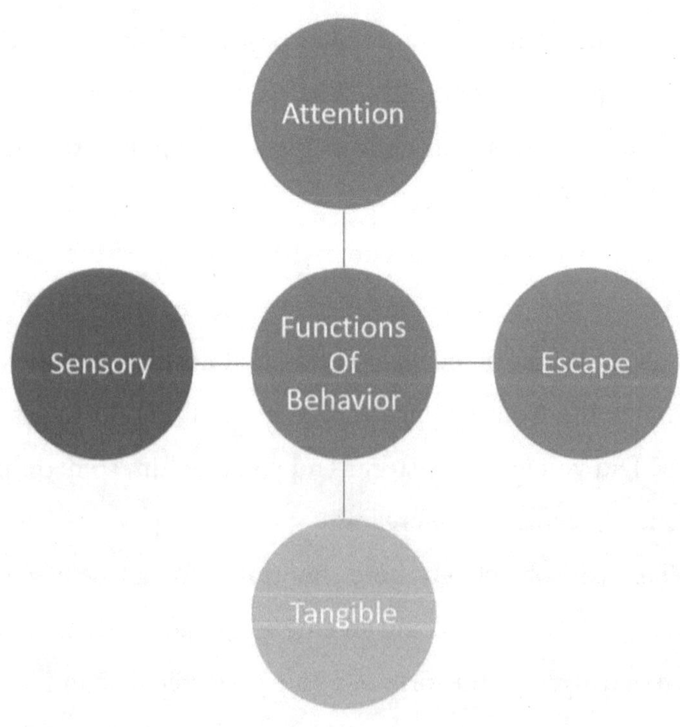

During the assessment stage, an interview with caregivers will typically provide an insight into challenges faced by the child and the family in general. Once the child starts attending therapy, the functions of behavior become quite apparent. In some cases, though, a more elaborate methodology may have to be set up to determine the function if the reason is not clear enough. How does this help the child? Intervention strategies to best mitigate a behavior of concern are implemented by determining the function. I'll give an example: Let's say a child engages in several avoidance-related behaviors such as crying, leaving the place, or throwing items around as soon as he is asked to complete homework. Our aim is that the child will be able to communicate "I don't want homework" instead of engaging in potentially harmful behaviors toward himself and/or others. In this example, the function of behavior is the same in both cases (the challenging behavior AND the replacement behavior): avoiding work—only the way it is expressed is different. So whenever we plan for a replacement to any challenging behavior, we want to ensure that the function of the behavior remains the same. So far, so good?

That was all about the established research, chapters from a textbook, contents from the parent training sessions, and a snapshot of a typical behavior plan. At the crux of all this, though, is your beautiful child, more than ABCs and functions. How are you going to figure out the best way forward when some challenging times occur after school, over the weekend, and during the holidays? Are you going to help your loved one or be worried about ABCs? Of course, you help your child first, but you also keep your eyes open so you can retrace the events and have an idea on:

What upset my child? What was he doing? What was said or done after?

It is really critical for us to be able to look at these stages objectively so we know the potential triggers. Too many times, we hear something like "There was nothing happening; he started acting out just out of the blue." This translates to "We couldn't see what triggered the behavior. Maybe the child wasn't feeling well. Maybe he got too overwhelmed looking at the work. Maybe he got too hot or cold, or he was bored with the activity." Something happened for sure, and we will need to be alert, especially for our kids who are still learning to communicate functionally.

At home, in natural settings, it is very difficult to follow a behavior plan the way it can be done in a controlled environment such as a classroom or a clinic. We may as well write "withhold attention" in the behavior plan if your child is seeking your attention in inappropriate ways (asking excessive questions, demanding your presence constantly), but it is quite difficult to carry out at home, especially if there are other siblings or you are multitasking with your various responsibilities. As such, ABA should be able to help you where you need the help—so if your child is showing more challenging behaviors in the home setting, that is where therapy needs to take place. In any case, during your training with the supervising BCBA, these issues need to be discussed and trained in detail. A home assessment may be conducted to observe and be fully acquainted with behaviors in a specific setting to adequately plan for successful intervention.

Rishi's Story

The doctor's office visits were in a league of their own. Rishi had frequent ear infections that required antibiotics, and that sadly meant we had to see the pediatrician often. Some weeks were back to back and the nurse would joke, "You guys almost live here!" The unpredictability of wait times in various areas of a doctor's office is particularly of great consternation to any of us, but to accomplish the same with Rishi was another story. And this was an era before smart devices. Let me repeat that: BEFORE smart devices. So without any phones or tablets to our rescue, it was just the husband and I taking turns minding our kid in what seemed to be an interminable wait in the waiting area. Our name was called, we were relieved, we would get to the examination room, and then after a brief chat with the nurse, we would wait—again—until our doctor showed up. Rishi would be literally all over the place during this whole time. The general waiting area was a far more demanding setting to monitor him, with other children and their parents and the exit doors. It was easier to wait in the smaller patient room, even with a general lack of toys or books. The biggest advantage was that we had privacy once we were called in, so we could be ourselves.

Waiting for an indefinite amount of time always had us on the edge. I feel in our minds we used to do a silent countdown for the inevitable blast off. We almost never visited some public places with uncertain wait times such as a restaurant. Takeout was our way of doing things, or we would wait for family to visit us so we could leave the kids in their safe care and declare proudly, "Oh, it's for here" in the restaurant.

We had already been kicked out of a hair salon due to hyperactivity during the wait followed by intense screaming and crying at the sight of scissors. We caused extreme inconvenience to other guests, we were told. We could have his hair cut at home or someplace else (no specific recommendations there), but just get him out of their chair and out that door, we were told. We did do that—walked out, purchased a buzzer, and gave Rishi a haircut at home—his dad hug-holding him while I somehow cut patches of hair; awfully irregular and clumsy, but at least it got cut.

You know how they say that the days are long, but the years zoom past? As I look back, snapshots of moments float by in front of my eyes ... those times when internally I was screaming but externally had to have a calm, even smiling, face ... when Dad was on travel and I was busy with Rishi's infant sibling, and he used the walls as his writing board with his favorite numbers (5 and 9) slapped all over with markers ... the stranger knocking on our door to inform me that small toy pieces were scattered all across the street from the right side of the house; maybe I could have a look ... the incessant water play flooding the kitchen or bathroom, and a denial of access to it leading to a meltdown ... the constant hiding of food in the pantry and Rishi ingeniously sneaking it. It felt like a never-ending game of Whac-a-Mole: you get one thing down, another pops up; you somewhat get that taken care of, and the third rears its head! It was an incessant stream of "Now what do we do?"

And then came the big behaviors that are very concerning to all parents.

The emergence of aggression and self-biting occurred around age seven, roughly coinciding with a relocation. The two years that followed were the longest and most frustrating two years for us as far as Rishi was concerned, for the most part. One of the most significant triggers of aggression was the word "no" spoken in a high pitch, typically to redirect him from an activity or to undo an error while working on academic tasks. Self-biting occurred during such times: when he was by himself, or when the sister cried, or during an unplanned time. To us, of course, it seemed like all the time! A big dark callus had formed on his left wrist, the place he bit himself repeatedly. We were made aware that self-injury releases endorphins in the brain, giving rise to an anesthesia-like effect thus numbing any pain, so the probability of this behavior increasing was high, as we could see it ourselves.

We were anxious to reduce and completely stop this behavior and started home ABA services from a well-known ABA provider.

It is arguable if we saw any significant progress with this provider, so we switched and contacted another well-known center-based organization. We were advised to use "chewelry"—to calmly redirect his attention to the chewelry when he attempted to bite himself, and to prevent this behavior by making his schedule predictable and assisting him to verbalize his wants and needs. These strategies worked like magic! We started seeing a decrease, and within six months the behavior was completely extinguished. For the first time, we were exposed to real high-quality ABA service, and we saw results immediately.

Rubber Meets the Road!

This is the real deal—when we actually implement all that we have learned to make perhaps the most significant and meaningful impact on an individual's life. All of us have moments of strife, disappointments, anger, and happiness—the intent is to deal with our feelings in the best way possible, and communicate the same. We have mentioned before, that our intent as caregivers, clinicians, or teachers is to provide the self-management and self-regulation tools to help the child control impulses and to effectively communicate his feelings while retaining his own uniqueness and individuality. In this chapter, I will attempt to provide some practical strategies for events that may trigger some challenging behaviors and also address some commonly stated concerns from caregivers.

Our children feel very flustered by not knowing what is coming ahead. The uncertainty and unknown can be very unsettling for them. It is always a great idea to maintain a routine and have a visual or written schedule for them as many of you may already be practicing. We maintain a schedule at a school or clinic; it is equally important to maintain one at home and adapt it per the child's growing mastery. He may start with a visual, then transition to a verbal schedule, and finally make one of his own. For my child, I can now let him know verbally about events to follow in the day, and not have to use visuals anymore. I had a student who would maintain a written schedule for the day and check off each activity on the list as the day passed. These days, schedules can be on the device in form of apps with alerts and reminders, that are very helpful.

I also find it very useful to indicate events on particular days using a calendar. Earlier on, we would use colors to indicate my husband's travel itinerary so Rishi knew when Dad would leave and when he would return. Now, we can pull up the app on the phone and let him know of upcoming travel plans, school closures, holidays, or any other event that might be slightly out of routine.

Another concept difficult for our children to comprehend is abstract terms like "Wait a bit" or "Later," something that we casually say to indicate an indefinite time period. I remember I had told my student to "Wait a second" while I was grabbing some things from my desk, and he immediately responded, "It is over!" Sure enough, one second as a measure of time was over as soon as I had completed my sentence; but the problem was, I never meant it to be a second in the first place, did I? So lesson number one—mean what you say. If you are asking your loved one to wait, try to put a timer to it so it is finite. If you say first homework, then the TV, do grant access to the television. Let him know for how long, but it is better not to push more work and assume your child has forgotten all about the reward. He may not say it, but he will know, and the next time you promise a reward for work, you may observe non-compliance, as sufficient trust is yet to be built.

All inappropriate behaviors are essentially mediums of communication. Our children just need the right means to express their feelings. Functional communication assumes great value toward being an appropriate replacement behavior to behaviors of concern. When your loved one is having a difficult time, we can give him some time to de-escalate and calm down; but it is critical to pair that emotion with the right words: "I need a break" or "This is too loud" or "I want to watch Dora" or "I want to play with Mommy." Whatever the reason, that needs to be functionally communicated. Requesting wants and needs appropriately may be a difficult goal to accomplish for many of our learners—they have to be aware of their needs and then communicate these. However, this is what we can attempt to train as a lifelong learning process. We have to caution against making the learners prompt-dependent as we constantly remind them, "Use your words" or repeatedly state, "What do you want?" before they can verbalize their wants. (This is a goal that Rishi is still working on to build complete independence in.)

Remember the ABCs of behavior we talked about earlier? In the Antecedent (A) stage, I am attempting to proactively help my child to minimize those hard times. To me, this is the critical pillar that many of us may miss while planning behavior plans. If we do not follow through, it will not be efficacious. As a clinician, I am all about antecedent interventions to produce behavior change, so that the child is independently communicating his needs and wants *before* any maladaptive behaviors have occurred at all. Using a timer to denote work time, setting expectations of what is coming ahead, using visuals such as a choice board and first/then statements, providing work in chunks before the entire workload is presented, and practicing functional communication are all examples of antecedent strategies.

There are strategies that are implemented in the Consequence (C) stage as well that may impact the occurrence of concerning behaviors in the future. The first point to clarify is that the consequence in behavior analytic terms is simply events that follow a behavior; it has no implication of punishment[3]-related events. This is the stage where we implement positive reinforcements. Any item or activity that your child values greatly may be used to build the motivation for them to work for. Before starting a session, we would always let the child choose what they want to work for, so the decision has been made by the learner, and not a staff member. We may have bubbles, cars, swings, computer time, play time outdoors, dinosaurs, Barbie dolls—whatever is a high value item or activity, we will use! Clinicians may run a "preference assessment" to determine what the valuable items are for your child. You may also have seen the use of tokens as a form of reinforcement. That is surely a great strategy for some of our children. Delivery of reinforcements follows some very carefully laid out rules—it is not just dangling a candy for writing "A". This must be trained and understood clearly during parent trainings for effective usage.

To illustrate how this all comes together, I will lay out some very common questions and how you may use the strategies listed above. Please note this is a suggestion for caregivers only. Please consult your clinicians for a thorough intervention strategy for your child's needs.

	CONCERN	CAUSE	ANTECEDENT STRATEGIES TO CONSIDER	CONSEQUENT STRATEGIES TO CONSIDER
1.	I cannot get my child to sit and work.	Consider the ABCs. Is he bored? Is it a non-preferred task?	• Let him know it is work time using first/then statement (first work, then play). • Let him choose what he will be working on ahead of time. (Math? English?) • Give him a timer to denote the time. • Consider three problems at a time if the worksheet is long (chunk work). • Keep a visual break card handy if he needs to take a break.	• Praise every positive behavior. • Acknowledge appropriate requests (I want a break please, or handing the card). • If the work is not over yet, and the child needs a break, run a simple mastered task such as "Put the pencil and eraser away," and let him have a short break. Get back to task when break is over. • Let them know when it is time to resume work. • Teach him to sit and attend to any activity, a preferred and non-preferred, other than school work, as a skill. • Encourage appropriate requests (replacement behavior).

	CONCERN	CAUSE	ANTECEDENT STRATEGIES TO CONSIDER	CONSEQUENT STRATEGIES TO CONSIDER
2.	My child hits me if I do not give him what he wants.	Consider the ABCs. Does he get what he wants only after he hits?	• Set expectations—when he may get it and if applicable, for how long. • Set a timer. • Keep other engaging activities handy.	• Acknowledge appropriate requests and feelings (I know you are upset; I know it is tough to wait). • Model an appropriate response. Have him state request calmly before providing the item with praise. Use pictures to help communicate wants/needs. • Teach him to communicate appropriately and "wait" as a skill (replacement behavior).

	CONCERN	CAUSE	ANTECEDENT STRATEGIES TO CONSIDER	CONSEQUENT STRATEGIES TO CONSIDER
3.	My child bites himself if he does not get his way.	ABCs to isolate cause. Is it only when he does not get his way or during a free time as well?	• All strategies of #2 above. • Consider having appropriate sensory supports—things that are meant to be bit or chewed on.	• Calmly and quickly redirect to sensory item. • Model an appropriate response. Have him state request appropriately and then provide the item with praise. • Teach him communication of needs and wants (replacement behavior).
4.	My child is always on the go/ is bothered by what he wears/refuses to brush teeth.	Consider ABCs, but he may also be demonstrating sensory needs. Consult OT practitioner as well.	• First/then statement to denote work time and break time. • Timer as needed.	• Keep sensory breaks as per the needs—tactile, visual, movements. • Incorporate sensory play indoors and outdoors. • Teach skills such as biking, swimming, adaptive sports, etc. (replacement behavior).

Point to note: To teach "waiting" we may have to start with a few seconds and then build up for best results. Similarly we may provide frequent breaks in a session at the beginning and then start reducing those. It is very important to take the time to build, before we accelerate.

A question that confounds professionals and parents alike is how to redirect self-stimulatory behaviors. We are aware that the child is coping and regulating himself through repetitive movements; however, these actions may be a barrier for the child to learn in some instances. We may intervene to provide "sensory breaks" to the child at these times and then set expectations of appropriate behavior (per the activity or setting) when the break is over. Also, there may be some social situations in which expected behaviors may need to be followed, such as in a movie theater (if it is not sensory friendly), in a library, or on a flight. In these cases, I feel we must train our kids to have sensory breaks to help regulate before they can re-focus and attend. This break can be activity oriented, keeping in mind the nature of sensory stimulation the child is seeking. For a tactile child, it could be things they can easily carry, like Play-Doh, slime, fidgets, etc. For visual stimulation, there are calming bottles; for kids who are seeking body movements, ideal activities include rocking chair, a bouncy ball, swings, a trampoline, etc., whenever possible. At the least, walking or jumping breaks can be provided. That way, we have not attempted to eliminate any self-stimulatory behaviors, but we have functionally redirected when the child needs to attend and focus.

We are acting and reacting to various internal or external stimuli throughout the day. For all of us, behavioral principles such as the ABCs of behavior or functions of behavior work exactly the same way. Our consequences typically go beyond tangible items—a great conversation with a friend, meditation, some me-time, window (or browser) shopping, or volunteering for a cause may all act as highly reinforcing activities for us. Our aim for our children is just that—moving away from external reinforcers, contacting natural reinforcement, and enjoying the activity for what it is. To get there, we employ a mix of teaching strategies that are right for that child, based on his strengths and needs. Just as it is our job to introduce that mix, and adapt and modify as we go along, it is equally crucial to fade those extra supports as the child learns and masters the skills. Our best reward is when we are redundant in our child's life. That is when he is who he wants to be; we get to sit back and enjoy his success in his way and on his terms!

~~~~~~~~~~~~~~~~

AT A GLANCE:

- Challenging behavior is a mode of communication
- Understand the Antecedent-Behavior-Consequences of behaviors—the WHATs of the root cause
- Understand the four functions of behaviors—the WHYs of the root cause
- Goal: have appropriate replacement behaviors such as communicating wants and needs
- Strategies to prevent challenging behaviors proactively
~~~~~~~~~~~~~~~~

Remember you're the one who can fill

the world with sunshine!

—Snow White

6

getting schooled: the special of education

You're off to great places!
Today is your day!
Your mountain is waiting,
So get on your way!
—Dr. Seuss

Rishi's Story

"UNFORTUNATELY, YOUR SON doesn't show us that he knows. We can get nothing out of him." The teacher and speech therapist had collectively passed the verdict. *"He cannot do much,"* is what they were actually saying to me. *"Your words do not match his actions"* was the fine print.

Rishi had made huge strides in the first three years of early intervention. The teachers always had enough to challenge him a little and to push him to learn a bit more than what he would be comfortable with. They maintained a delicate balance there, judicious not to frustrate him, yet prodding enough that the push was gentle and did not come to a shove. Everything had to be taught to him bit by bit—asking for things, playing appropriately indoors or outdoors, eating, dressing, grooming, participating in social outings. Each time I would marvel at how easily and how well typical children picked up without needing to be deliberately trained. On the one hand, I was getting around to this notion, while on the other, somewhere in the back of my mind, I felt that the gap between his developmental milestones vis-à-vis the typically developing peers was narrowing and that Rishi would be mainstreamed into general education soon. Yes, he would need accommodations, but with the required supports in place, it would happen.

Then came a relocation.

I reached out to the parent support groups in my current place of residence—many of the members were confidantes by now—to help prepare for the impending relocation. The one consistent voice I heard across the board was: Don't go! Services cannot and will not be matched. Nowhere close, even. In reality, though, there was not much of a discussion on this topic. We were not really in a position to maintain two establishments in two different parts of the country. With me being a stay-at-home parent of a special needs child and a demanding toddler, it was a no-brainer that we as a family had to be together as we relocated, no matter the level or quality of the new services. We bid goodbye to our beloved friends, prayed desperately that I would be proven wrong, and started getting settled in the new place. The house was bigger and newer, and Rishi definitely liked the space. The complex grounds had beautiful picnic areas and walking trails that we were excited to explore.

The self-contained classroom Rishi had been placed in could not be more in contrast to the one he had transitioned from. It seemed every entity in the classroom—students; staff members; classroom furniture; sensory equipment, including a trampoline and swings; and sundry classroom materials were all desperately jostling for place in that space. Visually, too, it looked extremely busy with charts and visual icons dotting every space in the wall, swings and classroom decor hanging from the ceiling, clamoring for some attention. And like a shroud over this packed space hung darkness. The ceiling fluorescent lights had been turned off. The natural light from the window was blocked off by heavy dark curtains. The three little lamps strewn around the class struggled in vain to illuminate the entire room. My heart sank as I took all this in apprehensively, wondering how this would go.

We got admission formalities completed in the zoned elementary school and realized the start time was pretty early in the morning. Therein was our first hurdle. It was extremely difficult for Rishi to wake up early enough for the bus, and after a few tardies, the school bus service was canceled. That eased the problem; however, a bigger concern stared at us. Rishi came back from school irritated, cranky, and upset on most days. The child everyone celebrated just a few months back was a shadow of himself now. He started exhibiting aggressive behaviors—hitting others when upset, biting his own wrists to the point that they had become black in one spot with a huge callus forming, and no matter what we did, he always seemed agitated. In a few months, the refrain I started hearing from teachers, paraprofessionals, and the speech therapist was, "He doesn't show us anything at all!" I would receive emails and phone calls from the school with complaints on his behavior. I was getting disturbed and deeply frustrated with this, trying to figure out what was going on. I really wanted to get to the bottom of the thing that was making my child so unhappy.

Rishi's new teacher was cooperative and wanted to help, though she expressed her doubts on his learning capabilities and adequate resources in her possession to effectively arrive at a solution. She was courteous enough to suggest I come in for an observation in the classroom one day, when, following a meeting, I expressed my anguish at all the changes I was seeing. My presence in Rishi's classroom had always triggered a complete meltdown for him on all previous occasions. He liked to have things in order, and my presence was the anomaly in the classroom—Mom belonged at home and not at school. This, however, was the very reason his previous teacher had encouraged me to come over on every occasion that parents could come in for (class parties for various occasions mostly), but it would break my heart to know that just the sight of me would ruin it for my little guy.

I warned his current teacher of this, and she made sure I was well hidden behind a divider, blocked from Rishi's view, while I observed. Circle time was on, and Rishi rocked his body and made sounds during the entire thirty-minute-plus circle time, seemingly in his own world, and completely tuned off from the proceedings. They were going through days of the week. and the teacher was calling on her students one by one to respond. It was Rishi's turn presently, and she called on him. I was very apprehensive whether he was paying attention or would say anything at all. It was a pleasant surprise to me when he responded correctly, and this pattern repeated two or three times more during the entire thirty-minute block. Even when he seemed absolutely immersed in his own little bubble, rocking his body and making verbal noises, he answered every time he was called on. I came out of the classroom with hope and renewed purpose—Rishi was learning in his own way, even with a lot of environmental conditions not quite aligning for him. He was showing his teachers all he could do. It was for them to identify the pulse and teach him the way he learned.

School of Thought

The decision for schooling for our kids can be fraught with worries and deep anxiety. Our lives revolve around our children, and a tad extra if a child has special needs. We get used to our own antenna being completely in sync with our child's needs.

To be away from our child, who may not yet be communicating effectively, and us not being able to anticipate or fulfill his needs in a timely manner, gets very worrisome. To add to that, adjusting to the dynamics of the school campus, finding our child's place in an inclusion classroom or with other potentially high needs children in a self-contained one, and efficiently navigating the complexities of special education can be very agonizing. Then there is that B-word—bullying! The fear of getting bullied, of the child's dignity not being maintained, and of him being the one to stand out in a crowd for reasons not always bordering on the positive can be daunting. It is definitely a decision that every family needs to make for themselves, and there is no right or wrong answer in that consideration.

Much of this following section may seem like a preaching to the choir for some of us. As parents of autistic children, we are well aware (and then some) of the school systems and the nitty-gritties of them, if our children attend public schools. However, for the benefit of all readers, here is the structure of the special education system in very broad strokes. Free and appropriate education is a right of all students. In that regard, special education provided in our schools is intended to address individual differences and facilitate learning for all students by providing a range of accommodations (factors that affect HOW a student learns) and modifications (adjusting WHAT a student learns). A student is placed in an individualized education plan (IEP) after diagnostic assessments have been carried out. A suitable placement will be identified within the various programs available in the special education department. These programs are structured, keeping in mind the needs of the students they will serve, from least restrictive to the most restrictive setting. Typically what that translates to is that a child may be placed in a general education classroom with only select accommodations in place, accessing the curriculum at his grade level, to cite an example of a least restrictive setting. Or it may be a self-contained classroom with a high student/teacher ratio, adequate accommodations in place, and a curriculum accessed at a prerequisite level, as an example of a most restrictive setting. In between these two setups, a variety of programs may exist that are blended in nature—taking in elements from both, customized to student's needs, to maximize outcomes for the learner.

Students may also be placed in a 504 program, referring to Section 504 of the Rehabilitation Act of 1973. Each student in the 504 program is diagnosed with a disability, and his education is supported via accommodations provided to him in a general education setting. For the purposes of this chapter, our discussion will be limited to students availing of special education services in schools through individualized plans and other related services to address their unique needs.

While scouting for schools/districts with good programs, the obvious question is "How do I find one?" It is impossibe to have such a checklist but some variables that may help define the quality of a special education program may be briefly enumerated as the following: varied programs available to best serve all students with learning differences, ample opportunities for inclusion, adequate staffing to maintain low staff/student ratios, suitable and frequent training for staff members and caregivers, access to best practices in teaching, and investment in high quality educational resources. Over and above all this is a term we are not only familiar with, but also have lived it: "A special education unit is just as good as its staff members." A passion to teach, a commitment to students, a high ethical and empathetic compass, and excellent intuition are skills that set one staff member apart from another. These are variables that money cannot buy and skills that are seldom trainable.

A Class Act

"Student success," "optimal growth," and "achieve full potential"—how many times have we heard these terms being used to describe a special education program? I can imagine a lot of you nodding! It always makes me wonder if we even fully realize the scope of these terms as we throw them around. What performance metric have we established that will reliably measure true "success," other than academic grades? How much or how little would be deemed "successful"? What is "optimal"? What comparative studies have we held to determine that a particular strategy was "optimal" for the student? What happens if it was not? And the classic "full potential"! Are we really claiming that a student will reach his fullest potential in a few months? And then what after that? How many of us truly believe that we have reached our "full potential" yet? (We sure hope we haven't yet, right?) There are too many rhetorical questions and too few convincing answers. There really is not one matrix that will suffice to establish quality benchmarks. I will attempt to break down the structure of a special education unit, the importance of Individualized Education Plan or IEP meetings, how goals may be written effectively, and the kinds of accommodations that may be provided so our learners are helped to the maximum extent possible.

Academics are building blocks to our child's future, and hence, it is imperative that the seven-plus hours spent in school are used constructively. Some schools may provide an opportunity to tour the classroom. In the post-COVID-19 world, that may look different, but overall we should keep some salient aspects in mind. While this is in no way an exhaustive list, it is meant to provide you with a broad idea of what to look out for in a special education unit as you make your decision:

- **Clear communication:** Talk to the diagnostician, case manager, or administrator, but most importantly, the teacher. Use that pinch of salt for whatever sounds too good to be true!
- **Individualized supports in the classroom:** Is there a schedule for every student? Are accommodations in place? Are assistive tools provided, whether pencil

grippers or speech devices, so that students may learn better? What is the student/teacher ratio?

- **Program details:** What assessments are being used to determine current functioning levels? What curriculum is being followed? How are teaching strategies being individualized? How are data being collected? Are the main domains of student functioning—academics, behavioral, social—being addressed throughout the day?
- **Other supports and services:** What are opportunities for inclusion? How about community instructions? Will there be field trips? How may skills be generalized across settings?
- **Collaboration with other service providers:** Are speech therapists, occupational therapists, music therapists, adaptive physical education teachers, et al., active in the program? How would coordination of services be carried out? Are you able to express concerns and hear back from all professionals working with your child?
- **Training:** Is training provided in best practices periodically to staff members? What are the opportunities for parent training sessions?

I doubt any of us would answer "yes" to all of these questions, but overall, we may have a certain percentage in mind as the criterion for program excellence. If some deficits can be overcome with one-on-one meetings and collaborations between school and home, that would be the best possible outcome. Some other learning aspects may be introduced at home as well, especially any learning that is best carried out in the natural environment.

Arguably, the most stress-inducing event in a special needs parent's life is—yes, you guessed right—the IEP meeting. This is an annual exercise that involves various stakeholders such as parents; teachers; other service providers including speech therapists, occupational therapists, etc.; the case manager/diagnostician; and an administrator to determine and assure placement of a student in the least restrictive setting as he pursues his education. This meeting provides an opportunity to review current functioning levels, goals already mastered, a new plan for the upcoming year, and any supports required to fulfill those goals and objectives. As the IEP committee comes to a consensus, the possibility of an extended school year is also discussed in the meeting. An extended school year is offered during the summer months when students have an extended break with the aim of maintenance (or, no regression) in skills learned during the school year. The IEP is a legal document, which means that careful consideration must be placed to fully understand this process and thereby be in a position to advocate for your child in an informed manner. There are professionals such as an educational advocate who may be present in this meeting to help navigate the process and help establish the requested services. There are also several training and guidance opportunities provided to families by various parent support organizations to educate and inform on the vast complexities of the process.

Personally, each year that I would attend my son's IEP meeting, I felt an incredible responsibility (and stress) that my actions would set another stepping stone in my son's life and prayed that it was in the right direction. I always found strength to have my husband by my side to navigate through goals, services, and service hours for yet another year, and I would completely rely on his exceptional communication skills to have a smooth meeting. As a family, our personal endeavor has always been to work closely with our child's teacher for the best for our son, and it has worked for us. We strongly believed in open communication with the teacher instead of brewing distrust in our minds. We found straight answers and a collaborative stance when we kept the communication channels fair, honest, and completely focused on our child.

Learning to Build

I consider myself fortunate to be able to sit on both sides of this table in multiple capacities—a parent, a teacher, or a supervising BCBA advocating for my client. Each of these experiences has brought in its own nuance, and I will attempt to share my perspectives on some key areas. As a parent, academics often seem to be the primary cause for worry. In a way, this is the easiest and most familiar yardstick for us to gauge our child's performance at school. However, this is what I firmly believe and always have structured programs around this belief: I have to first make sure that the child is available to learn before attempting to place heavy demands. (As you read on, the meaning of this statement will be clearer.) Hence the goals that we as teachers plan for should include targets and skills across domains that are functional, connected, and will carry over across settings. For instance,

BEHAVIOR	SOCIAL	SELF ADVOCACY	ACADEMICS
Johnny will sit in one place and attend to tasks for ___ minutes	Johnny will work cooperatively with one peer during a shared activity	Johnny will request help	Johnny will complete 20 addition problems during math block
Johnny will gain attention of adults appropriately	Johnny will take turns with peer	Johnny will request a break	Johnny will demonstrate comprehension by responding to WH questions
Johnny will transition across settings with one prompt	Johnny will share materials with peer	Johnny will indicate termination of activity with "all done"	Johnny will identify and state features of five landforms, body systems, etc.

All of these goals are closely interconnected, all appropriate for an educational setting. A lot of it may actually be occurring naturally in a school day; however, it helps to understand that we all are aware that these specific goals have to be targeted by service providers across settings.

The IEP goals must be specific, measurable, and time bound. For instance, a goal may read: *Johnny will complete 20 addition problems in math with 80% accuracy for three consecutive days.* We have indicated what Johnny needs to do and by when and how progress will be measured. In this, we may also indicate whether this task will be independent or prompted, and the level of prompts if applicable. A goal statement like *Johnny will solve more math problems* is not an example of an appropriately written goal. Further, the goals should be attainable. We want to challenge our children, but we definitely do not want to overwhelm them with too much too soon. So, if your student today is unable to sit and attend to tasks for five minutes, can we have a goal that they would be trained to engage in tasks for twenty-five minutes by the end of the year? Check! If the student is unable to complete one worksheet today, can we have a goal that they would be able to do so when trained? Check again! If the student is not able to participate in shared activities with peers, can we have a goal that they would? Yes, check that! The time taken to achieve these goals may differ per student—for some students, these goals may be attained within a month, and for some others it may be a school year. The important thing is that it will be accomplished.

Maintaining a balance in the number of goals is another critical factor. Quantity definitely does not equate to quality. We want our students to learn and demonstrate mastery in class and ensure those skills generalize across settings (home, community, after school classes, etc.) and across people (caregivers, friends, other instructors, siblings, etc.). We also must ensure that the learned skills are maintained over time that is, they do not regress/forget. We must probe mastered skills from time to time toward that goal. For our learners who are accessing curriculum at a prerequisite level, the academic goals must be very functional and relatable. Our learners often end up learning skills in isolation, and the information sits like little islands in their minds. As much as possible, we, as teachers, should be able to connect those dots for them and help them see the bigger picture. Consider, for example, the skill for addition and subtraction. If we connect the concepts to money, then a whole new world of learning opens up. Now they know what it means to add and take away and why we must learn the concepts. We can train addition and subtraction skills in class and generalize the skill in the community. This essential skill will very easily maintain over their lifetime. I call this Functional Academics—making learning contextual and relatable to everyday experiences.

Our learners who may not require extensive modifications in curriculum may require a variety of accommodations to successfully get through the day. I had a student who was brilliant in math and science and required minimal support in those classes; however, for English, language arts, or theater, which required abstract thinking and creativity, he struggled a great deal. For another student, a grade of 99 was reason enough to punch a hole through the wall in frustration of missing the one mark.

Yet another student would shut down seeing a worksheet full of written words—just the fact that he would have to read through all of it to complete it was too overwhelming. Some strategies may help in this regard:

- Access to a **quieter environment** when overwhelmed. A library is quiet, too, but there is much visual stimulation in the library, which may prove to be distracting and unsettling. A smaller, quieter homeroom with adult supervision for one-on-one assistance as needed would be helpful.
- Being able to **verbalize feelings** and being guided to accept and acknowledge them can be very helpful. Once that is done, students may come up with strategies that they feel would be most helpful in mitigating their stress and anxiety. Self advocacy is an extremely powerful tool that we must encourage every step of the way.
- Being **rational about feelings** and being abreast of a worst-case scenario would help being in control of emotions. Is it really that bad, or am I thinking it is so? A trusted adult or mentor may greatly help in this process. Understanding and acceptance go a long way as coping skills for the future.
- Adjusting the **response effort**—the amount of effort required to complete a task—can be a very simple accommodation. Can the worksheet have five problems that are

> spaced out so it does not seem too much all at once? Can breaks be implemented so the required number of problems is completed with a slightly longer time granted to submit work? Can someone read out questions during the tests?

In the IEP meetings, accommodations are always discussed. I have found it to be very helpful to discuss goals and all supports that may be in place ahead of time with my son's teacher. This saves time during the IEP meeting, and it gives parents the time to discuss their child's progress with other professionals who they may not have the opportunity to meet frequently. It also helps to be prepared with some questions ahead of time. It is never too early to start thinking of long-term goals for the child—this is the time we can set the ball rolling by asking pertinent questions, understanding the process when the child ages out of the school system, and having a fair idea of what preparations may be in place to best serve our child. A positive home/school connection can be an anchor to a child's progress. No matter what the case may be, we should never lose sight of our one and only goal: working in the best interest of the child. Things sort out rather easily when this simple objective is not overlooked.

~~~~~~~~~~~~~~~~~
~~~~~~~~~~~~~~~~~

AT A GLANCE:

- Special education: IEPs, 504s, accommodations
- Preparing for an IEP meeting
- Functional academics: some examples
- Quality over quantity
- Collaborative and strong home/school connection

Open different doors. Anything can happen!

—Mary Poppins

7

taking care of business: personal care

You'll never be bored

When you try

Something new.

There's really no limit

To what you can do.

—Dr. Seuss

Rishi's Story

THOSE DARNED "NOODLE chips"!

Made of chickpea flour, these were gluten-free, deep-fried delicacies that look like hash brown shreds. You could get them in different thicknesses, but Rishi liked the super fine consistency. He just loved these! He could eat them any time of the day, in almost unlimited portions. It would be rather impossible to either deny him the chips or restrict to a small portion. And thus ensued a cat-and-mouse game with me coming up with new hiding places in the pantry and him seeking, displaying the most ingenious problem-solving skills while doing so. He always scored, mostly right around dinnertime, and my mind raced to work out another new place. Eternal sunshine of the hopeful mind, I would muse wryly.

Rishi was a picky eater during his toddler years, and that lasted until about five years of age. He was picky about textures and would gag at the slightest crunch in his food. I primarily gave him over-cooked rice and vegetables so he could swallow without having to chew, almost like baby food. I particularly recall how much I tried to get him to have a sandwich—peanut butter and jelly, Nutella, grilled cheese—everything a child is supposed to love, but to no avail. Eventually, we started therapy with a feeding therapist. Within the first two months, he was eating fried rice, noodles, and a jam sandwich, foods that I had struggled with for over a year. In the course of the following week, the therapist approached me apologetically and said that she was really embarrassed to charge us, as she practically did nothing during the session. Rishi would come in, open his container of food, eat, and walk out. Things had not changed much at home yet, so she offered to let us use that room any time we wanted to, since he was so compliant with food there!

We needed Rishi to start getting independent at home. Rishi's pre-K teacher and home therapist helped us tremendously to generalize skills from school to home. In the course of six months, Rishi learned to eat while seated at the dining table and to use a spoon and fork, though he preferred using the fork over the spoon. He had a spot at the table, and he ate all his food there—meal, snack, ice cream, one cookie—whatever it might be, he knew to sit and eat. He was eating a wider variety of foods than before but still had very specific preferences—no sauces and no crunchy pieces in the food. He steered clear of small cut vegetables such as diced carrots, peas, and mushrooms. His dad, a great foodie, had never stopped encouraging him to take a bite of all the different foods at home. Rishi protested initially, but he soon realized that gravies (or popularly known as "curries") actually made the dry rice so much better. By middle school, around sixth grade, due to his dad's persistence, he dipped a chicken nugget in ketchup ever so slightly for the first time and barely licked it. That was that moment, folks! He didn't gag and he liked the added flavor, so he took the chicken nugget, dunked it in ketchup, chomped on it, and has never looked back since. Now he tries everything from sandwiches to sushi, dunks in the appropriate sauce or dressing, and eats every cuisine offered to him with great pleasure and delight. He can eat fish with fine bones and debone like an absolute pro with incredible dexterity. The process evolved over fifteen years, with persistence and consistent presentation of a variety of foods—but in the end, the transformation was nothing short of a miracle.

All About Picky Eaters

Picky eating or intolerance of foods is one of the most common challenges that caregivers worry about. Studies have suggested that children with autism are five times more likely to exhibit some type of food intolerance than their typical age peers.[4] A variety of factors may result in food intolerance, ranging from sensory defensiveness to aversion of the taste or texture of the food. Sometimes, it is simply too long and boring a task that children would rather avoid, just so they can continue on with their fun, more engaging activities. There may be physiological issues as well, such as acid reflux, underdeveloped oral muscles, or a gag-reflex condition that makes children feel that they are choking. In our field, we would always want to rule out any such physiological issues before proceeding with a behavioral intervention. A feeding therapist, occupational therapist, or ABA therapist may help with food tolerance intervention or may co-implement goals across settings.

From the behavioral perspective, food tolerance protocols in the clinics require patient and sustained implementation in cooperation with caregivers. We typically start with one food at a time (say, broccoli) and go through a step-by-step process toward getting the child comfortable with the food item—holding the food, touching it to the lip, touching it to the tongue, chewing without swallowing, and finally, picking up the food and eating it. Some children may breeze through the steps, and some may take longer to master. For many children, parents have reported that they needed to follow the protocol for one food option, and when another new food option was offered, the child showed no resistance and tried it readily. The dilemma one faces with food is that we cannot let a child go hungry, and pushing a food that he is resisting may be very aversive and traumatic in some cases. We should really be very careful about how much the child can tolerate and work closely with caregivers for this target. There are numerous research studies with scientifically validated strategies that have improved food tolerance without being aversive, and many of these studies may be sourced from the internet from reliable websites. These strategies may be utilized to make the process gentle and smooth.

One of the ways to minimize aversive experience is to pair the non-preferred food with a really preferred food as you start training. So if chicken nuggets do the trick for your child, then pair the broccoli with the nuggets. Encourage a bite (or touch, depending on the stage the child is in) of broccoli first before a bite of the nugget. Again, it is a slow process requiring a lot of patience, and your child's therapist would be the best person to list out the steps in detail. Personally, we continued encouraging our son to try new foods consistently—if he showed interest, we increased the variety in that category, such as a steak, grilled chicken, burgers, Philly cheese steak, chicken sandwich, etc. If he resisted, we backed off, often giving him the tiniest bit to try just so he would not be overwhelmed. Eventually we ended up with an "okay with us" green zone—the bare minimum that would be okay with us if he tried. Over time, Rishi started indicating the foods that he did not want (like mushrooms and peas), and we were thrilled to hear his voice in those instances.

There is just one thing I feel I want to caution parents about. How many of us run around different stores making sure we are getting the exact same food in the exact same package? We secretly pray to the grocery gods that they do not revamp the flavors, the packaging, or even worse, discontinue the item. How many of us consider the kitchen of the golden arches to be an extension of ours? My point here is: this all may be good with your child, but what about when he grows up? What if those foods are discontinued, or God forbid, some health issues crop up? How much would you like for your child to eat the same food as everyone else seated at the dining table without having to stress? Yes, they do grow up before we realize it, and whatever may not be appropriate for him long term may need some rethinking and training now. The sooner the better, if there are no physiological needs that are barriers to the food tolerance process.

Grooming, Hygiene, Taking Care of Self

Life skills incorporate the essential skills of daily living that are critical for an independent and self-sufficient life. Commonly referred to as "activities of daily living," the skills are best trained in the natural environment, with natural outcomes. You cook, you eat the food prepared—natural environment and outcome. You shower or bathe, you are clean and tidy—natural environment and outcome. You dress per your choice, you look spiffy—again, natural environment and outcome. Why do I keep mentioning "natural environment and outcome"? Well, these are skills that one would perform every day throughout one's lifetime. We may start training with M&Ms as reinforcement, but we would not expect that to last a lifetime, right? It then becomes very important for our children to contact natural reinforcement for activities—that is, we should not have to always reinforce with an item each time they perform a routine task. Training these skills and fading external reinforcement may be carried out with specific ABA-based strategies, some of which I will list out.

There are some common characteristics among such tasks as showering, dressing, cooking, etc. These tasks require multiple steps to be performed in a sequence. One step follows another, and no step may be skipped. We can modify the tasks to suit the level of functioning or age of the child, but those steps will still need to be completed. ABA strategies prove to be very effective in training this kind of sequential multistep activities in a structured and logical manner. The first strategy we may implement is called "Task Analysis." This means that we will break down the activity into various steps and train one step at a time. Let's start with an activity like the very loved peanut butter and jelly sandwich. In order to make the sandwich, we may list the steps as follows:

1. Get two slices of bread
2. Put them on a plate
3. Get the peanut butter jar
4. Get the jam jar
5. Get a butter knife
6. Spread one slice of bread with peanut butter
7. Spread the other slice of bread with jam
8. Put them together
9. Eat!

Now we can do this for various activities: washing hands, making a bed, brushing teeth, packing a bag, etc. We can even break apart tasks; for example, showering may be divided into subtasks such as shampooing the hair or soaping the body to provide that extra assistance toward independent completion of the activity.

Task Analysis presumes that the child will be able to follow each step, understand what to do, and carry out each step. But what if our learner is not there yet? What then? No worries—we have "Chaining" to the rescue! Chaining also requires the task to be listed like Task Analysis, but we will teach one step at a time and then move forward. For our PB&J example, we listed nine steps. For the Chaining process, we can train the steps forward, in the natural sequence of 1 through 9, or backward, from 9 through 1. Several factors may determine what we choose to do for a child, and I will not bore you with that. This is best discussed with your clinician, who is working closely with your child. The main thing I would suggest is to always consistently follow through, without any confusion to yourself or your child. My son learned to dress himself with a backward chain: I would help him pull his shirt over his head, and he would pull it down. That way he got dressed quickly, and the activity was completed. He learned to make a bed with a forward chain, learning the steps sequentially—he would start off by completing the first step, and his therapist or I would finish the rest. Over time he has learned to independently carry out the whole activity—whether dressing or making his bed.

While training, we may find that the child is not able to execute each step with perfection. The bedsheet might not be fully straightened, the peanut butter might not be spread evenly, or the shirt could be scrunched up. The step has been completed, kind of, but not quite appropriately yet. No worries again. We will "Shape" the behavior, or we will slowly train to make it perfect. If your child has already gone through several steps to complete a task, then a further demand to demonstrate perfection might be overwhelming for him at that time. But for the next time, the task is not so new anymore. That is when we will place the demand to do a little better, and so on. We may have to show him exactly how and keep training until the desired outcome is reached. This shaping strategy is also very commonly used in language development and articulation in children. We take what we can get (for example, buh for bubble) and refine it as we go along, so it is kept achievable for our children. It is important to keep a balance in our work demands for our children—we do want them to learn, but some children will need to be taught in a slow and steady manner. Patience is definitely a virtue!

How does this all fit in? Let's say your child is making a sandwich as a snack—he knows each step, but he might get confused about the sequence. Use Task Analysis to help with the sequencing. Does he need to learn how to dress? Consider a Chaining procedure to teach the steps. Is he learning to fold laundry? Maybe a shaping strategy will help—he will start with approximate attempts until he perfects it. As always, check with your child's clinician/teacher for specifics. My goal is to give you an overall idea of how these strategies work in unison.

Since we are in the realm of chores, there is another task that works well as part of skill generalization. Prerequisite mathematical skills of matching and sorting can be functionally used in a variety of chores and vocational skills in the natural environment. Putting groceries away in the pantry, match and sort; clearing out the dishwasher and putting items back in their designated place: match and sort; separating laundry: match and sort; separating trash and recycling: sort; packing party favors for kids: match and sort; tidying stationery up: match and sort (pens/pencils/markers etc.). Skills learned in one environment have practical applications in another, and it is essential that our children make these connections so their learning is meaningful and the overall outcomes are relevant.

Controlling variables in the structured setting of the classroom or clinic can be done much more effectively than in the natural environment of home. Unpredictability is the name of the game at home, especially with young children, working parents, and a busy bustling household. All children do well with schedules, and children with autism in particular can be very independent and thrive with schedules. The schedules can be visual on a device in an app, or they may be written on paper. These schedules may be used in creative ways, customized to the tasks for which they are intended—for example, a chores schedule can indicate "to do" and "done" tasks, helping to keep track of chores completed, reinforcing accomplishments, and seeing the list shrinking. Who doesn't like scratching things off a to-do list? These visual schedules may also be handy while implementing the Task Analysis and Chaining strategies discussed above. Instead of verbally instructing, we can follow a written or visual representation of steps to be completed sequentially. Again, the steps can be checked off as the child proceeds independently through the sequence. The hard work here is upfront while setting up the schedule and training it, so it is followed appropriately. Once the child learns it, he is likely to follow along with minimal prompts, and over time, he may no longer even need those.

For us, visuals were an absolute must-have during the initial years of training Rishi. One of the major concerns for us was when he raided the pantry right around dinner. The home ABA service provider had created materials to train us on various strategies to tackle this problem, but the solution of having visuals of his preferred snacks on the pantry door was simple and very effective. It required us to honor Rishi's request for the "noodle chips" right before dinner if he requested appropriately using the visual. Over time, we started implementing a time delay with a timer: "In five minutes, you can have the chips, when the timer rings." Slowly that got to "First dinner, then chips." Somehow, holding that visual of the chips (a small actual photo of the item) assured him that they were indeed forthcoming. You will recall that building trust is an essential part of the pairing process. Rishi required reassurance in two aspects: that the chips were still present even if he could not physically see the pack; and secondly, that he would be given some to eat if he requested them. The picture served the first purpose, and our structured intervention built the essential trust factor.

We found as time passed that the habits that he picked up early on—putting his belongings away, sitting at the table to eat, and rinsing dirty dishes before placing them in the sink—have endured, and he does these without needing any reminders. In fact, he is the one picking up after us now! In the training phase, though, each step was accomplished one at a time with the help of visual supports, a schedule, and timers. Rishi learns fast when there is a consistent structure he can follow and understand. Initially, we had to keep things simplified and at bare bones, but over time he has learned to face life as it comes—tolerating last-minute changes, bearing uncertain wait times, accepting other peoples' choices, giving up preferred items, or patiently waiting for a preferred item or activity, is delayed. He is agreeable through it all as long as he is provided with a simple verbal guidance on what to expect.

Snapshot of Bedtime and Potty Training

It is the end of the day, and you are exhausted after being on the go for what seemed to be an eternity. Bath time is done, and the book is chosen. You are ready for the story and the gentle tuck-in. You just want your child to get to bed and fall asleep so you can wrap things up and hit the bed yourself.

Easier said than done, is it not?

Recent research suggests that almost 80 percent of children[5] diagnosed with autism spectrum disorders have trouble falling asleep and staying asleep. This is more probable if the child demonstrates repetitive behaviors, anxiety issues, and/or sensory disorders.[6] This sounds all too familiar for families who are struggling to attain that elusive good night's rest for their children and themselves. This issue is one of the dominant areas of concern for most parents, regardless of a child's cognitive or functional level. Just as with picky eating, ruling out any neurological concerns would be step one in this process as well.

Rishi had difficulty staying asleep more than falling asleep as a baby. Some days would be both in tandem, but most nights, he would be up and about for two or three hours straight. No matter how dark the room, how soothing the music, or how active the day, he just could not stay asleep through the night. We stuck it out when he was a toddler, but as soon as we were able to, we had him on a supplement to help with sleep. At the same time, we made modifications to his diet, as that was a popular suggestion from other parents. The diets did not do much either for his sleep or overall behaviors. Rather, he would not like the taste of the food so he would remain hungry, which resulted in "hangry" issues constantly. We later consulted his neurologist and found that Rishi was not intolerant to any food items that we were denying him when following the special diets. From then on, at the advice of his physician, we reintroduced a normal diet in phases, and after some trial and error, found one medication that helped him stay asleep through the night, which in turn, regulated his mood significantly.

Overall, though, a bedtime routine has to be very consistent. Electronic devices have been found to be detrimental and overstimulating, so it is best that they are turned off at least a half hour before bed. Visual schedules help a lot, too—the "bath, book, and bed" troika is easy to consistently follow. The usual checks are essential—the room is dark, a preferred stuffed toy for snuggling is offered or maybe a snug fitted blanket (yes, that is a thing, like a fitted sheet concept). In case he does wake up at night, have a monitoring device handy and some extra mattresses that could provide a cushioning effect to safeguard against falls. As best as possible, childproof the room to avert any potentially harmful or dangerous situations. Also, try to avoid any preferred, reinforcing activities at this time. The room is still dark, we are trying to fall back asleep, not engaging in any activity of choice.

It is also helpful to have a consistent wake and sleep routine. As I write this, I know I am guilty of not following this very well. During the holidays and inevitably during the summer months, I get to witness the results. That is when we resort to various activities in the daytime—swim, bike, walk, etc.—so Rishi will be naturally tired and will want to sleep. In the training stage, the child should be trained to sleep in his own bed and to be independent while sleeping. I am very aware of the cultural differences that could be a factor, but here is how I have approached this previously: in general, if your child has no problems sleeping in his own room, remaining in his own bed, and falling and staying asleep—in other words, if you as a parent have no sleep concerns for your child—then if he requests to be with you, you can easily make that call. If, however, your child is demonstrating sleep challenges, then it is best to spend time jointly in some bedtime routines such as lying down together and reading a book but exiting after the tuck-in.

Another major concern for parents is toilet training. My son's training—having a bowel movement while appropriately seated in the toilet—was accomplished by the time he turned one year old. For that feat I take no credit—that is all due to my dear mother. I only maintained that learning. Getting rid of the diapers during day and night time was harder, and my mom would have done that, too, had we not relocated. These are topics of extensive research, but to jot some main points, for any toilet training to be successful, the key is consistency with times. We add or induce the motivation factor by making it an awesome feat to have emptied in the toilet. At the clinic, the training requires us to have the child sit on the toilet at scheduled time intervals for certain durations. For instance, the child will sit for five minutes every thirty minutes. We have a potty timer on, produce highly reinforcing items such as the coolest toys that are given only on successful toileting, and top it all up with an animated celebration.

Obviously, this is time consuming. Many times, other targets may have to be put on hold or reduced just so this schedule is maintained. It is also essential that the same routine is followed at home with the same time frames (per our example: take the child every thirty minutes, make him sit for five minutes, and provide access to a highly preferred item on successful toileting). This makes it easier for the child to know that diapers will no longer help and that he has to take care of business properly. I would also strongly recommend that toilet training is commenced very early on, so inappropriate habits do not form. Referring to my rule of thumb: if a typically developing child of the same age is demonstrating an essential life skill, then we start training our child if that skill is not in his repertoire. It is much harder to train an eight-year-old to have bowel movement (or urinate) in the toilet instead of a diaper than to successfully train a two-year-old. It is much harder for the older child to get used to sitting if he is used to standing up and voiding. Such a demand will lead to some inevitable challenging behaviors, which in turn becomes difficult on caregivers, and the whole protocol may be abandoned in favor of maintaining peace in the household. This is understandable, but at the same time, it must be kept in mind that for an essential life skill, and the earlier we can start, the better. Home ABA providers can help implement this goal as well as any of the activities of daily living discussed in this chapter. Trust me, the rewards you will reap are boundless.

~~~~~~~~~~~~~~~~

AT A GLANCE:

- Picky eating/toilet training: consistency is key to success
- Have routines and schedules
- Use Task Analysis to break down tasks
- Use Chaining procedures to teach a task
- Use Shaping procedures to make it perfect

If you want something done, you've got to do it yourself!
—The Little Mermaid
~~~~~~~~~~~~~~~~

8

siblings, friends, and the endless holidays!

If you never did,

You should!

These things are fun,

And fun is good!

—Dr. Seuss

Rishi's Story

"MOMMY," SOBBED MY then three-year-old daughter, "please, please can I exchange my brother? He does not talk to me, he does not play with me like [my friend's] brother does! He hits me and screams and cries. Please, Mommy, please!"

I recall that day as if it were yesterday! Rishi's sister—a bright, cherubic child—did not mince her words. I held my weeping baby girl, gently rocking her and soothing her while my heart seared in pain. I felt the pain of knowing that she and her brother would never know how precious the brother-sister bond was and would never understand the significance and warmth of the bond through various festivities in our culture—and no, baby girl, there is no exchange here. "God chose you to be a sister to your special brother as you are the most precious one, my darling," I explained. "Look at your awesomeness that *you,* not anyone else, get to be the sister of a special brother. How amazingly cool is that?" She looked at me through her tears, trying to make her mind up whether all this was truly special. She decided it must be since I seemed so excited, and then she scurried on to the doll that needed her immediate attention. My heart, though? It decided to speak through my eyes.

Rishi's immediate cousins, two wonderful girls and a cool little boy, are always protective and highly indulgent with him. Sadly, however, all of the cousins' interactions are greatly limited by geographical distances, living across three continents and seeing each other in the flesh only every few years. Each time they do get together, I would imagine them to have conversations. I wondered how it would have been. Would they discuss studies; tease each other with girlfriends or boyfriends; or debate movies, shows, games, or books? Would he be a sports fanatic? Would he be an introvert or extrovert? My questions may remain unanswered, but it is always so heartwarming to know that Rishi loves them all, and he expresses himself in his own way. I would catch him looking through the photographs and home videos from years past with all of them together. When did physical distance create a distance of the heart? I would muse. They all understand the language of love, in all its purity and supreme majesty.

At the time Rishi was in elementary school, around seven years of age, each family in our social group seemed to have a family structure like ours, with a son and a daughter of our children's ages. Getting to someone's house needed long preparations from our end with Rishi's favorite toys, edibles, and sometimes a change of clothes packed separately. If the drive had been of a reasonable time, approximately fifteen minutes, we were good. If it was any shorter, we would drive around, stop at a store to buy a hostess gift, and then proceed to the friend's house so Rishi would get to ride in the car for a while. This was to avoid an unpleasant episode of him crying as we stepped inside, at once trying to greet our hosts and calm our child, all due to an inadequate car ride. Weekend social visits to friends' houses had my daughter in spirited play with her peer group and the boys running around in energetic make-believe games while Rishi, exactly their age, stood out painfully from the group. He would sit with us and the other adults, rocking himself, making noises, and being transfixed with opening and closing the DVD tray. He would then take off and explore the hosts' refrigerator (for desserts), pantry (for potential snacks of interest), or the bathroom (to take a lick of the toothpaste).

The contrast was so stark and so apparent that I almost always wanted to decline invitations. It made me gloomy, painfully aware of differences, and very vulnerable. The "whys" had no answers and left a melancholic strain in my heart, and the frustration inevitably spilled onto other things. In reality, I never declined the invitations though. Seeing my daughter play with her friends acted as a balm. She did not have peer play opportunities at home, and I did not want to rob her of these moments because of my selfish emotions. Over time, our close friends became familiar with the drill with Rishi and were very patient and supportive—they would walk him around for the "tour," and they would put us at complete ease. I am so grateful to them for not excluding us from the social do's and for always making our family feel at home. Things have improved with Rishi over the years to an extent that now we can inform him of a "party house," and he will be thrilled—jumping around and wanting to hear more about whose house we will go to and what we will do. Our group of friends is our big family here—our son's social skills and etiquettes have become sharper over the last ten years, thanks to their welcoming hearts and homes. As I write this, I realize that this may have been the start of the journey called "acceptance"—for us, for all of our friends, and for our family. This is not at all an easy journey—it is continually evolving, but highly rewarding.

Siblings and Friends

Siblings of special needs children often end up caught between worlds of being a caregiver and a peer model, and companionship most certainly gives way to caregiving responsibilities. Working parents especially may tend to depend on their typical children to be their eyes and ears in their absence. It becomes the utmost priority for parents that the needs of the typical child may not be overridden by sometimes the more pressing needs of the special child. I have witnessed the conflicting emotions and the delicate vulnerability of the typical sibling with my own family and through those of some of my students and clients over the years. The myriad feelings and emotions that typical siblings may go through are often widely contrasting. They may feel jealous of the attention their special needs siblings demand, be disheartened with the lack of interactions that they observe, feel highly protective of their sibling, and feel a resentment toward adults if disparate expectations are in place for the siblings.

As parents we try our best to acknowledge and alleviate the confusions, making sure to spend one-on-one time with our children in a way that fulfills their needs in their own ways. Many families face the challenge of keeping up with the needs of an honors student or a star athlete along with a high needs special child. I have admired so many parents who have juggled their roles effortlessly, completely exhausted, but never let up advocating for the diverse needs of their children to the fullest extent. Especially if the typical siblings are younger, spending time exclusively with them becomes critically important. As they grow up, they need to be secure in the knowledge that parents are fair and free of bias. As the needs of the typical children evolve over stages of their lives, a constructive and robust sibling support group may make it easier for them to share and be encouraged to learn from others in a similar journey. Going by my personal experience, I have yet to find such a support group, nor have I received a particularly enthusiastic response from my daughter when I have broached the topic. Having a healthy support system in terms of friends and family may just suffice for now.

My daughter has grown up with therapies and classes for her brother. She accompanied her brother and me to every session and got busy with whatever books and toys she found in the waiting area, many times late into the evening. Never did she complain or fuss. Whenever we had babysitters, they would be amazed that the three-year-old knew everything about her brother, where things were in the kitchen, and how the evening schedule should be followed to keep her brother engaged and comfortable. I could not be more proud and more grateful to God for the wonderful caring sister she has been. However, at this three-year-old phase (Rishi was six or seven), she would also tease and pester her brother, just for fun—mostly with silly gibberish, but this would always end up being a trigger for Rishi. A natural childhood teasing phase manifested in far reaching ways for us—Rishi started getting annoyed with any little girl around him. The self-contained classrooms had students from three grade levels in one unit, so there would be younger girls in the class. I would always let the teachers know to keep an eye out in case anyone got loud and Rishi became agitated. At home we would explain and admonish our daughter and separate the two of them as best as possible; however, the occasional silliness continued, the response from Rishi (knocking his sister on the head) persisted, and all of this resulted in inevitable chaos and pandemonium.

So how may we start building positive interactions between siblings? Interaction with siblings and friends would be a subset of general social interaction, though the nuances may be very different. Procedures such as pairing, shaping, and play strategies have been discussed in earlier chapters, but to recap, just as we talked about pairing a new toy, we can also pair a sibling during play time. They can engage in a shared activity or game, both of which need to be highly preferred. The pairing process can start with the sibling engaging in play for a few minutes and then leaving before your special child feels the need to protest. Initially, your child may still protest this unwelcome intrusion. That is fair enough—we must prepare him in advance for the plan and keep the interaction short. It is always a good idea to provide appropriate words to your child if he is not yet fully verbal: "I don't like it," "Please leave," "I want to be alone," etc. This is a great way to incorporate functional language in natural opportunities and situations. Self advocacy is a critical skill for our children, and interactions with siblings provide a perfect opportunity for these social skills.

The interaction time may be slowly increased so we may go from barely tolerating each other's presence to actually meaningfully engaging in an activity. The biggest thing to always remember with behavioral therapy is that there is no magic pill here—it is a process that requires consistent implementations. Consistency sets a structure and helps the child learn. I personally feel there must be a balance in our approach when we facilitate these interactions. On the one hand, siblings can act as a typical peer, modeling expected interactions; on the other hand, if our children make their voice heard, we must honor that as well. In such cases, it always helps to find a shared interest between siblings that can be built on. In our family, these are water-based activities, arcade games, bowling, traveling, dining out, and relaxing family time at home with a movie. All of these activities need an adult to be around for overall supervision and monitoring, but the siblings would be engaged on their own in a collaborative manner for the most part. If either of them did not want to engage with one another and wanted their own space, that was absolutely acceptable as well.

Interactions with friends may require sustained exposure with engagement in activities of shared interest. It is, of course, imperative that both children are interested in the activities and willingly take part in this process. In our case, we found a group of special needs families from a similar culture when Rishi was in his early elementary school years. We would organize picnics, birthday parties, and general get-togethers outdoors where our kids could run around and play. They were timed events. We would bring preferred food and beverages, and we all could be ourselves without feeling judged, feeling lonely in a crowd, or being singled out. It was a feeling of community for us and helped each of us through some really tough times. As Rishi grew older and matured, he started enjoying inclusion opportunities with his peers in the middle and high school, and he looked forward to these events with them. These events ranged from athletics (Special Olympics chapter) to Best Buddies programs at school to various other social events. If you didn't know better, as an outsider looking in, you would think Rishi was not actively participating and was in his own bubble with the peers around him. You wouldn't be further from the truth though. He participates, follows along, and has a blast in his own way, even if that does not conform to the expected or "normal" body language. He would stay on until the event wrapped up, say his goodbyes, and then leave.

This is not unique to him. All of my students in the high school where I taught exhibited a similar pattern of engagement with peers. Their faces lit up when they were with their peer buddies and reveled in their attention, their company, and the activities they performed jointly. My students were at varying levels of verbal communication, but that was the last and least of a barrier in any of this. They may not have provided the eye contact that we deem socially appropriate, or they may have rocked their bodies or made noises that we would feel compelled to stop and redirect. None of that hindered any activity or came in the way of fun and pure glee. Whether it was participating in a day or overnight summer camp, being in the school team in athletics, or hanging out with their typical buddies over the weekend, they were like any other teen, enjoying themselves in their own way as they lived their lives.

Recreation

Are you rubbing your head already? You know you are not alone in wanting to tear your hair out trying to figure out what exactly would keep your child occupied in a purposeful way. I know how much we struggled with appropriate leisure activities when Rishi was younger. We even enrolled him in "recreational therapy"—basically a space filled with a variety of toys with adults facilitating structured play with siblings or a peer. Before we delve deeper, let us keep in mind a unique characteristic about leisure or recreation. Recreation is essentially an unstructured time when the child has to keep himself engaged and occupied with an activity that he finds appealing, without requiring constant adult attention. The child needs to be independently occupied in the home setting in particular—the parent has chores to be completed, another child has to be attended to, dinner has to be cooked, and errands are to be run. It becomes rather impossible to provide one-on-one supervision and monitoring for every waking minute, so appropriate recreation and leisure skills assume great significance.

Meaningful recreation often becomes a challenging skill to train, and I am always asked two very important questions on it: "Why can't they engage appropriately?" and "How will they engage appropriately?" I will attempt to break it down, starting with the "why." As we know, whatever we do, we derive some reinforcement from it. The degree of reinforcement will vary from task to task. For instance, when I watch a thriller movie, I derive positive reinforcement that is higher than a horror flick. So when I am watching a movie by myself, I will almost invariably choose to watch a thriller. Now this changes a bit if another variable is thrown in: the company of another person, be it a spouse, friend, or partner—someone's company that I enjoy and value. So for me, I would watch a horror-action flick simply because I'm with my husband—his presence has amply compensated for the lesser reinforcement I would derive from the horror movie. So the choices we make are a product of the interplay between several variables, all providing some forms of reinforcement in the natural context.[7]

This same interplay is in effect for our children as well. But the choice of activities that they derive maximum pleasure out of may be to spin items, make noises, repeatedly press a key on a keyboard, script a line from a show, or engage in vigorous physical movements. They are deriving immense pleasure from these activities and getting reinforced in high degrees from these activities. The problem is that these activities may not be socially appropriate or functional. Another problem is that we can rarely relate to this as we likely will not derive any reinforcement from any of these activities ourselves. And the bigger problem for us is that the child is not in one place, quiet or involved in anything we perceive to be fruitful.

That leads us to the next question: How do we mitigate this? Right off, this question poses a dilemma: are we to redirect and stop every pleasurable activity, however non-functional, simply because we, the adults, did not think it was appropriate enough? What, then, of the child's own individual choice—did we disregard it just because we could, and he did not have the agency yet to express and advocate for his wants? I wish to take a balanced approach toward a solution. There must be time during the day that your child may engage in activities of his choice, without adult redirections (unless, of course, we are talking about a harmful activity). We may make this access timed—so that would be a fair deal for both your child and you, the parent.

Next is the question of introducing variety in leisure activities. In the natural development process of a typically growing peer, would he engage in a variety of play activities? That answer is a no-brainer. So for our special children, this process will have to be a structured process to train, if we keep in mind the age appropriateness of leisure. Would I, through a process of trial and error, need to probe the interest and inclination of the child toward a particular activity? Yes, I sure would. Would I, however, push a leisure activity on the child even though he may not like it or have no interest in it? No, ordinarily I would not, though there may be some exceptions, as we will examine shortly. So we will have to think of ways to start broadening his interests and likes. We need to remind ourselves that this will likely be a long-term process, requiring consistent exposure to various objects or activities of potential interest.

One important thing to remember here is: the activity we are presenting as "leisure" or "recreation" has to have the same reinforcing value as any other non-functional activity that your loved one may be engaging in. Simply speaking, coloring (an intended replacement leisure activity) must be just as fun as spinning items. If it is not, then the child may comply with the request for a minute or two, but he will not engage in a sustained way. Most parents indicate that their children's interests are very limited—"they don't like anything besides X." Yes, they don't like it YET—but they may once they find out how much fun it is. If your child is interested in watching a Disney show, for instance, you can get toys, books, or games (board and electronic) relating to that show to start widening the scope of play. You can also take that concept for just about anything he likes. Libraries are a great resource for books, ebooks, toys/games, electronic devices, etc., during this exploratory stage, so we don't go bankrupt purchasing them. Thrift stores can be treasure troves for a lot of these resources on a budget as well.

As you can well imagine, exposing your child to new materials will take a time investment from your end. If you have home ABA therapy, this will be an excellent goal for the therapist and your child to work on. In the initial training phase, Rishi's home therapist would expose him to a new activity for a very short time before giving him his preferred activity. He had a "leisure schedule" with specific websites he needed to navigate and engage in for five minutes each. A variety of websites were introduced so he would sit and engage starting from five minutes, going up to twenty minutes. Rishi always thrived with visual supports in a structured learning format, and he quickly got the hang of it. Since we are talking about leisure, electronic devices were our mainstay. The YouTube channel is loaded with songs of Rishi's choice, and the computer's hard drive has tons of family photographs and videos from vacations. There are some preferred websites of simple games that he accesses. Wii bundles, sensory items, and bouncy balls (tennis balls, mostly) add up to the main leisure activities for Rishi. As you will see, most of these can be easily carried with us wherever we may wish to visit or travel. He does not need a visual schedule for leisure activities anymore and is quite adept at being at leisure independently. We are nowhere close to where we want to be, but like with everything else, the work is definitely progressing.

~~~~~~~~~~~~~~~~
~~~~~~~~~~~~~~~~

AT A GLANCE:

- Pairing, shaping strategies to facilitate sibling play
- Peer play opportunities can be a subset of social interactions at school/clinics
- Importance of leisure and recreation skills
- Structured leisure training
- Important to honor self advocacy

Some people are worth melting for!

—Olaf, Frozen

9

out and about: community outings

Be sure when you step,

Step with care and great tact.

And remember

That life's a great balancing act.

—Dr. Seuss

Rishi's Story

FINALLY, OUR BIG day was here, and we were already running late.

Food is the *raison d'être* of our lives. Okay, that is a bit of a stretch, but only a bit! It really is that mood-lifter, happiness-bringer, making memories 'round the table kind of catalyst. And the thought that we had not stepped out as a family to dine in a restaurant for the past few years was emotionally crushing. We had to find a way to make that happen.

With an infant and the four-in-one Rishi, it seemed to be a distant dream anyway. But to be fair, in hindsight, we had been laying the groundwork with Rishi. Food tolerance was much better now, and we had been training Rishi to sit and eat at the dining table instead of me spinning around the room to have him eat. With both of these new skills under our belt (or rather Rishi's), our first steps in eating out had been to the neighborhood McDonald's for a quick meal. We ordered Rishi's favorite item on the menu—a chocolate sundae—sat at the play area, and dined. We planned ahead—our dinner would be completed at home, but there is always space for ice cream, right? Rishi was thrilled. We had our fingers crossed for the sugar rush, but we just went with the flow. It was amazing! Rishi barely had to wait for his treat, and we chose our spot by the play area to minimize disturbance as he loudly enjoyed his frozen treat. We couldn't have been happier!

Revved by that positive experience, we were now ready to crank it up a notch. Today was the big day. We all would have a meal (not just a treat) at—hold your breath—Fuddruckers. We would be met there by his home therapist, and we would introduce Rishi to the next level in dining. We needed to be seated appropriately, wait for food to be ready, and navigate stations to customize each order. We did the best we could, but an hour-plus later, we were glad to be heading home. Rishi was overwhelmed with the many new experiences and had a difficult time waiting at the table for the food to be ready. He got under the table on multiple occasions. The noise level at our corner was definitely elevated, and so was the activity.

Our adventures being out and about in the community were manifold, just as you may be going through as well. Rishi would inevitably leave our side and run from us at the grocery store, fixated on pulling open the freezer doors at the frozen aisle and then slamming them shut. Occasionally, he would pick up a bag of M&M's or Kit Kat or a crazy bouncy ball and would get into a tantrum if we did not buy the item. Doctors' visits with uncertain and really long wait times were a challenge. So were haircuts and visits to shopping malls, each for its own reasons. And we did not even dare to visit the library or think about going out for a movie. It would always amaze me how much our behavior as adults is governed by others' perceived reactions or thoughts. We were sensitive about whether we were judged and what strangers were thinking as our son wiggled around screaming on the floor at the checkout aisle. It took time and practice to convince ourselves that those strangers' judgments, if any, were of no consequence to us. This was easier said than done, but it was essential to get done, nevertheless.

Today, participation in none of these tasks requires even a fraction of second guessing and minimal planning from our end. While I ponder over how that was accomplished, I feel I was delightfully unaware of any conscious process when we were going through all this. If anything, nothing seemed to be working, progress seemed very slow, and new challenges had to be tackled on a regular basis. I feel I had a very simple question that I asked myself each time a challenging behavior reared its head: Would it increase or decrease his quality of life as he grew up? If something did not work, such as not being able to dine out or go to the movies, I had to find a way to make it work the best way possible. I feel sharing concerns routinely with teachers and therapists almost always helped us brainstorm, and interacting with other parents helped me look for classes and get a process started. In the pre-social media days, there would be calls to parent support groups, and the occasional meet-ups with other parents further helped me to figure out the road ahead, even if the outcome was pretty much up in the air at the time.

In the Public Eye

If someone had asked me "On a scale of 1 to 10, how stressed are you at the thought of being out and about with your child?" my answer would have been "10" at one point in time but close to "0" now. Yes, it is stressful, and no, you are not alone. It is very normal for us parents, teachers, and caregivers to feel the anxiety of the unknown. Now imagine how incredibly hard it must be for your child: the sensory overstimulation, the unfamiliarity of just about everything around him, and the inability to express what he is feeling. With every challenging behavior being a mode of communication, when there is a meltdown, aggression, or running away episode, your child is talking to you in his own way: "This is too boring, Mom"; "This is too bright/too noisy for me—I'm getting a headache"; "I recognize this candy/

toy in all the blur and I want that NOW"; or "Get me out of here, Mommy!"

Again we face a dilemma here. Where is the line between listening to their voice when they protest and redirecting to teach an appropriate "replacement" behavior? Are we listening to our children as long as they are saying what we want to hear? I sure hope not! Concerns are growing that somewhere, as parents, teachers, or clinicians, we are trying to make neurodiverse children indistinguishable from their typical peers, and that their voice is getting obscured, along with their uniqueness. I feel that appropriate communication—whether to state a need or a denial—must be a priority so our children can advocate for themselves in a way that everyone can comprehend. Do remember that communication is not just verbal—it can be a picture exchange method, an assistive device, simple visual boards, or whichever way the child is able to meaningfully get himself "heard." We must immediately honor all appropriate requests if they can be carried out. If the request can be met with a delay, then it must be acknowledged and clear expectations set as to when and how that may be possible.

As an example, my son would often communicate displeasure by crying and aggressing if he did not like something. From the parent's perspective, it was certain to me that I did not want my child to scream as a means of refusal. I kept urging his teachers and therapist to "Just teach him to say, 'No, I don't want to.'" I simply wanted my child to learn, just like any other child.

As a professional, though, I realize how difficult the concept of negation can be for some of our children and how extremely demanding it may be for some children to learn to say "no" as a self-advocacy skill. This goal is a work in progress for my son; but we have found a way to hear his voice by presenting questions with choices instead of an open-ended "yes/no" kind of question. We will have to find a way to ensure self-advocacy every step of the way so the voices are not obscured, even when they learn and sharpen the skills over a longer period of time.

Getting Out

Community outings are an essential life skill to learn, a necessary step toward a higher quality of life that will ultimately prepare the learner for a life of independence. These outings require a multitude of skills in various domains and maybe a life-long learning process for some of our learners. Our job is to keep exposing them, maintaining a careful balance that the outing is not aversive or unpleasant to our child. In our case, we needed to find suitable ways for our child to express and communicate and to understand that we cannot get candy or a toy every time we came to a store. We also had to find ways to minimize the sensory overstimulation as the first steps.

One of the key elements of a successful community outing is the amount of planning involved. We try to anticipate the potholes and pack the necessary cushions to soften the blows.

We need to do all of this proactively, so we can be prepared when and if the moment hits. I am sharing some strategies that have helped us over the years and some others that I may have used with my students. Of course, as always, this is by no means a comprehensive list—this simply provides an idea on how we may structure our intervention strategies for our children to learn. For this purpose, I will use eating out at a restaurant as an example. This structure may be applied with appropriate modifications for any community outing of choice.

We are preparing for an infrequent and less familiar activity, a unique set of expectations, conditions such as a high level of noise, high levels of activity, the presence of strangers, uncertain wait times, and preferred and non-preferred food and all this in an unfamiliar environment.

Examples of skills involved at the restaurant by domains:

- **Communication:** When ordering, expressing feelings.
- **Social:** Greeting hosts and servers.
- **Behavioral:** Regulating emotions in an unfamiliar place, waiting for food, sitting at the table appropriately.
- **Life Skills:** Using a public restroom, displaying good table manners, using a conversational tone of voice.

An important point to note here is this: the skill examples mentioned in the Behavioral and Life Skills categories may first be taught in isolation and then generalized to a different setting (community setting). If we focus on the generalization aspect during the community outing and not the training of the skill itself from scratch, it will be easier on the child and on the parent.

Resources to carry along: you can consider a backpack for your child with a variety of goodies, including activity books, small toys, travel games, sensory toys, etc. I am not a fan of Play-Doh for these outings due to the mess it may cause. The other major concern is the contamination factor with the Play-Doh being placed on multiple surfaces, etc. It is also a good idea to carry along quick activities—many children do not want to leave an activity unfinished.

Beginner, intermediate, and advanced activities, based on the level of support needed:

Activity: Going to a Restaurant

	BEGINNER	INTERMEDIATE	ADVANCED
Step 1: Choosing the Place	• Buffet at the start of dining hours: Zero wait times, immediate access to food. • Fast food place if your child can handle a slight wait. You can keep him engaged in the play area.	• A chain sit-down restaurant: Call ahead for any special requests. • Team tag: One of you can arrive ahead of time and place the order; the other can come in slightly later so as to minimize the wait time.	• Varied choices: Take turns in selecting cuisines to teach acceptance of others' choices. • Prepare for an unfamiliar cuisine with a backup plan that is mutually agreed on.
Step 2: Prep Time	• Show and tell: Tell your child and show pictures about the upcoming visit—where you are going, what to expect, and what you would be doing (social narrative or social story). • Ideally, this should be introduced some days before the event. Build up the excitement! • Go over behavioral expectations—goals he has already mastered.	• Tell him: You may now fade out or use visuals as needed. Let him know the schedule closer to the event. Let him know where and when you are going. Talk about the menu and discuss order choices. • If it is a familiar place, talk about a previous visit. • Set behavioral and food expectations.	• Schedule it in: Discuss the time and place. Discuss the menu. Ideally, you are looking for compromise—you will try to accommodate everyone's choices and teach acceptance of non-preferred options as well. • Set expectations on behaviors, budgets, food choices.

	BEGINNER	INTERMEDIATE	ADVANCED
Step 3: During the Visit	• Connect the dots: Link the visuals to the matching real-time occurrences. • Refer to the schedule and check off the steps already completed. • Specific praise on the expectations that you had set. • Praise effort throughout. • Food should act as a natural reinforcement/ reward. • Encourage appropriate communications throughout. • Take pictures. • ENJOY your time!	• Go over the schedule and review the steps already completed. • Specific praise on the expectations that you had set. • Praise effort throughout. • Food is the natural reinforcement/ reward. • Use natural opportunities to encourage communication. Talk about the food: categories, (desserts, drinks, appetizers), healthy vs. unhealthy, colors, etc. • Take pictures. • ENJOY your time!	• Natural learning opportunity to learn etiquette: dressing, eating, excusing oneself appropriately to get up (toilet, etc.). • Talk about future work ideas—ushers, servers, chef, cleaning staff, etc., and what they do. • Specific praise on the expectations. • ENJOY your time!
Step 4: After the Outing	• Talk about the visit, referring to the pictures. • Encourage recalling the food eaten, the drink chosen, the delicious dessert. • Take note of what went well and what could be better to adjust for the next time.	• Talk about the visit by presenting what, where, why, who, when, and how questions. • Refer to the pictures for recall. • Talk about likes and dislikes. Tie in emotions. • Take note of what went well and what could be better to adjust for the next time.	• Talk about likes and dislikes. Encourage self-advocacy skills and clearly communicating feelings. • Encourage a rational and logical approach. • Encourage a self-evaluation of the outing and strategies to adjust to make it even better.

You can replicate this structure for visits to the shopping mall or grocery or other stores. Some components will change, and since there is flexibility with time in the stores (no waiting for ordering food, serving, etc.), the best way to go about it would be to keep the visits short at first and slowly increase the duration. Also, have a plan about what the goal is for the stores, for example, a list of things to buy. For us, we would add in Rishi's favorite item (Kit Kat, M&M's, or a toy) at the end of the list of three to five items. It can be a visual list at first, then a written one, and finally, a verbal list, depending on your child's needs. In a restaurant, food is the natural reinforcing factor; in stores, it can be that added preferred item. In the mall, it can be to play in the play area or to have an ice cream before leaving. You can then start adding in a visit to one store, and then two, and so on. Over time, you will be able to limit access to these external reinforcements to every other visit, and finally, to what your family's rules may be. Personally, I ALWAYS let Rishi know what we will do and set that expectation. I use short sentences and count the activities on my fingers for multiple tasks. He is now able to follow verbal instructions and reminders and remember them.

For a visit to the library or movie theater, there is one added component: being quiet while engaging in the activity. As a family, we are now able to carry out all these activities with slight adjustments, though a loud laugh during a dramatically intense scene has baffled other patrons in the movie theater from time to time! We started with sensory-friendly shows before graduating to regular movie times with the four of us and then in a group with close friends. Rishi goes to the movies with his class friends, too, and that has also helped. Library visits commenced with time at a computer playing games and engaging in puzzles and other activities. The children's section is a bit noisier—so that helped for sure, as did a timer. The library here is by a very pretty pond. Rishi likes to throw stones into the pond, so we would follow up a successful visit with time by the pond. We still keep the duration short, and he is the biggest (and tallest) kid in the children's section, but who's complaining?

Visits to doctors and dentist add further components to this routine and expectations. Our current neurologist and pediatrician, both Dr. R., have been especially supportive and worked with us every step of the way. They have encouraged us, given us time, listened to us patiently, and comforted us with assurances. For these visits, I have followed the same strategies with Rishi. The pictures may have changed and the specifics of expectations during the visits may have been modified, but the overall structure has remained. Dentist visits are a bit more challenging for obvious reasons. The intrusive nature of dentistry makes many of us feel very uncomfortable. The noise level, sensations, and discomfort of the process are even more aversive for our special children. We were lucky to find a dentist who specialized in working with our children. She had several sessions for children to be familiarized with the office, had mockups of the process, and a visual social story to go over the steps. Ours and several other families benefited from these practices. We can try the modeling with prototypes, but we have to be able to desensitize our children to this process by a slow step-by-step exposure as required.

I am reminded of the saying, "When you meet one person with autism, you meet ONE person with autism," as I try my best to provide some overarching strategies. ABA is individualized for each child. My effort here is to share some common goals and targets that may benefit children and their families and help them to access a better quality of life. The critical thing here is consistency. No matter how challenging it is at first, keep at it. Keep going to places and doing things. Strangers may give you the eye roll, look at you as if a circus is on, or make you squirm. They are nameless entities in your life—their opinions do not matter. Your child totally does. Those strangers will not come to your help in your times of struggle, so yes, feel free to completely disregard them. Work through the difficulty your child is having and try to isolate the antecedents.[8] That will give you an idea of the factors that are too overwhelming for your child. The consequences will keep you aware of any trappings that may be inadvertently maintaining any behaviors of concern. Again, please always remember that challenging behavior is a mode of communication. You are helping your child make it better for himself. There is always a reason for your child to feel uncomfortable, whether or not you see it. You are trying to figure it out in the best way possible and helping your child minimize it.

A lot of my thoughts have been shaped by the words of Dr. Temple Grandin, who I regard in the highest esteem. She once mentioned that her mother held the same expectations of her as any mother would of her children. Dr. Grandin worked hard to meet those expectations (and surpass them beyond measure). I strongly feel that as parents, teachers, therapists, coaches, and clinicians, we need to have those dreams and expectations of our children and students. So many times in my personal and professional capacities, I have witnessed first hand the magic of expectations. Teachers and students have worked beyond capacity to accomplish goals that were dismissed by others. Many of these may seem daunting, and it may seem like years before your child can accomplish the goals. Still, please do not give up—the progress may be slow, but if there is a positive slope to that graph, you are on the right track. The slope of the graph may follow its own unique trajectory, but ride with it and enjoy every bit of that ride. Your child *will* surprise you and one day, when you reminisce, you will marvel at how far you all have come.

~~~~~~~~~~~~~~~~~
~~~~~~~~~~~~~~~~~

AT A GLANCE:

- It is stressful for children and parents to be out in the public eye
- Plan ahead, and use visual aids as required
- A variety of goals across domains may be addressed during community outings
- Expectations of each place will differ
- Training needs to be according to the unique features of the place

Venture outside your comfort zone.
The rewards are worth it.
—Rapunzel

10

going places: travels and travails

You have brains in your head.
You have feet in your shoes.
You can steer yourself
Any direction you choose.
—Dr. Seuss

Rishi's Story

OH, KEY WEST! You captivating beauty!

We are proudly smitten by wanderlust, and we look forward to our escapes as earnestly as we work hard to earn them. The bucket list is reasonably long and varied—travel places are selected based on art, architecture, food, or natural grandeur. A place read about in a book, recommended by someone, or seen in a movie—if it catches our fancy as a must-do, into the bucket list it will go.

Remember the climax scene of the movie *True Lies*? Schwarzenegger rocked the stunts, but what really caught our eye was the exquisite Seven Mile Bridge of the Florida Keys. It had been in the list for too long, and we waited eagerly to knock it off at the earliest opportunity. The holiday was planned during the Christmas break. Every hotel, every activity, and every authentic seafood restaurant had been meticulously searched and pinned. Sadly enough, the universe had other plans. Days before we were set to depart, I got into an unfortunate (and completely avoidable) car accident two blocks from our house, and I sustained some injuries that required immediate medical attention. We canceled our trip with a heavy heart, determined to make it to the islands as soon as possible. Fast forward two years, that time had finally arrived, and we were more than ready. Our vacation would start from Key West and we would drive north, exploring the islands in sequence as we drove up.

Key West greeted us well. We were instantly swathed by the balmy island air, invitingly warm and just a touch humid, as we exited the tiny but efficient airport. We fell in love with the aqua bluish-greenish water of the Atlantic, the island charm, the hip vibe, the colorful people, the fun street corners with touristy antics—the wait was so worth it. We were definitely on island time. We were determined to make the most of our stay as we soaked in the vibe and spirit of the place. We sauntered past beautiful cottages, surprised by the presence of iguanas lounging in a languorous siesta in the afternoon sun, the merry revelry around the corner, mostly around the clock. Hours passed and we exulted—until the moment hit.

The CVS pharmacy was at a busy and rather dirty street corner, swarming with tourists. Some last-minute tidbit was to be purchased. We all walked in, casually browsing and scratching our heads as we asked ourselves if we were missing any other item. It started with Rishi crying and hitting his sister's head. I looked at him, trying to occasion an appropriate request with a "Use your words" kind of phrase. The crying and attempts to hit escalated. I guided Rishi and his sister to exit the store as fast as I could while my husband wrapped things up. We glanced at each other; no words were spoken, but we were in perfect sync. At the entrance, though, the dam had burst. Rishi, overwhelmed by the experiences of the day, lay crying and rolling on that dirty street corner, even more busy and noisy in the prime evening time. Too many disapproving looks and shaking heads attempted to bypass our crying and aggressing child who was creating a foot traffic obstacle in that busy intersection.

My little daughter, embarrassed by the sudden unwanted attention, tapped on my arm and whispered, "Mommy, they're looking!"

"I know," I said, "Ignore them. Your brother needs to feel better."

We soothed our distressed child. As soon as he had started to calm down, we asked Rishi if he would like a break. "Break, please," he immediately echoed. Of course, you need a break. We used bottled water to wash his hands and face. My husband found an ice cream joint, and we sat and slowly exhaled as Rishi enjoyed his treat, relieved for the break he must have so desperately needed. We made a mental note of how to make it better for him.

We rarely pass up an opportunity for a getaway when we are all off for a few days—even if it means converting a day trip to an overnight one. Our holidays are primarily by the sea, since Rishi adores everything water. We are lucky to be in a place that is close to a beach city and temperatures are warm enough for almost a year-round getaway. Rishi loves hotels, too, the freshly laundered "white sheets, white pillows" being his absolute favorite. We always go over the dates and itinerary with him, no matter the duration of the stay. (We use the calendar extensively to familiarize him with comings and goings in general—be it a business trip of a parent, arrival of guests, impending social invites or scheduled school events, as mentioned earlier too.) For unfamiliar trips, we google the places and notable sights so he is aware of what to expect.

This has been a successful strategy so far. Progress in other related areas such as toileting, food tolerance, and dressing and grooming himself have eased and expanded our travels as well. We have traveled overseas and have been on a cruise. We have traveled by ourselves or with others. Rishi has been exceptional with demands placed during unfamiliar times. Despite planning for these vacations, there have been one or two exceptions. A similar incident to the Key West one occurred at the New England Patriots Hall of Fame Museum at the Gillette Stadium in

Foxboro four years back. The intense cold (it had snowed heavily in late March; we were over there for our "spring break"), the drive around the Charles River with some selfie moments, and finally to Gillette—my boy had had it by afternoon. This time he did not flop to the ground, but he caught me off-guard with the crying and aggression as we neared the gift shop of the museum. The armed policeman perhaps assessed the situation and was kind enough to let us hastily exit through the nearest door. The walk through the parking lot was challenging—it is so much easier to pick up a distressed child than to guide a distressed adult safely—but my husband stepped in and we managed. Back at the hotel, under a warm blanket, Rishi was a different person. We were snowed in for the next few days, just stuck in our hotel room, and he was a happy camper—no grumbles and no protests. He was happy with the people he loved, his own little universe contained in a room.

Off the Beaten Track

We discussed community outings in the last chapter, and much of the core principles remain the same while planning for a trip or vacation. What differs is the scale and magnitude of the plans. There may be an overall plan for the days that the vacation would last, and then a separate plan for each day. Every experience and activity is expected to be unique and one of a kind, involving unknowns. Referring back to the ABCs of behaviors that we had discussed earlier, we are heavily relying on the "A," or the antecedents (what comes before the behavior), as we plan and prepare. Our goal with planning is that we can be at a stage where our child would know and be comforted by what to expect. On our part, we are hoping that the realm of unknowns is brought within some bounds. We would then introduce some reinforcing items or activities during our day to acknowledge and praise the incredible effort of our child. For Rishi, these reinforcing items include chewing gum (as part of sensory support), music, frequent breaks, and access to highly preferred activities such as a beach or pool in between less preferred activities such as sightseeing. In the absence of water activity, we rely on preferred food during meals. Luckily, Rishi has a vast culinary repertoire now, and he is always able to find something preferred in any cuisine. However, we started at a point where we would always book hotels with kitchens and cook meals. As Rishi's food tolerance and acceptance increased, our food-related preparations during travel also diminished (generalization and maintenance of learned skills in action).

Along with preparing ahead, it is also important to continue to provide opportunities for your child to choose instead of you choosing for him. While you may be practicing choice making in any case, during a vacation, it may add a dollop of stress if the choice is not exactly feasible and you are not able to carry out the request. One of the ways to guard against this would be by providing options, all of which are feasible and doable at that very moment, much like a multiple-choice question format. A choice of clothes, which place to visit, a choice of seat in the flight or rental car, a choice of bed at the hotel, what food to eat (this can be a general burger or pizza question and/or selecting the actual order off the menu)—any time you can, have your child choose. The rationale behind this is manifold, but to focus on some of the main ones:

A. You are continually teaching and practicing self-advocacy skills.
B. You are making sure your child is just as involved in the vacation as the rest of the family, regardless of how well he may express himself.
C. It gives him a sense of control when familiar surroundings have undergone a sudden and very quick change.
D. He is more likely to willingly follow his own choice instead of being told what to do.

Grab the opportunities and provide options that are doable—this is a relaxed family time and must be enjoyed by all.

Hand in hand with decision making is handling responsibilities. Children do wonders when they are given responsibilities, and your child, regardless of age, can be in charge of a few things during the trip. The best way to start is with things that your child will be invested in, for instance, handling his own belongings. His backpack may be loaded with reinforcing items such as edibles, electronic devices, and sensory items; and essentials including chargers, medicine, clothing, wipes, and sanitizers. He can help pack according to his wants and be in charge of the belongings, replenishing items as needed and can carry it around. As he grows up, you can add items to this list—his suitcase, fun activities to plan, essentials for the beach or park, or a picnic basket. He will meet you where *you* want to meet him; just remember he is taking one step at a time. The escalator does not work and the elevator is non-existent!

Fly Away!

Two words: air travel.

This is enough to send many of us packing, right? Now imagine a twenty-hour-plus flight with children, one of whom is a special child. No thank you, you say? This, however, is a reality for many immigrant families here in the United States whose close relatives (including parents, as in our case,) are in their native countries. This trip has to be made, and over the last two decades, it has been a part of our lives every few years.

The first twenty-three-hour flight was the worst one—the experience of the long flight, not the services. I was travelling by myself with my infant son, completely ill prepared to travel with an infant in general. I don't know who cried more during the flight—Rishi or I—but after the never-ending hours (truthfully, minutes and hours have a mind of their own in the flight), the blob on the screen finally touched land. It got better each subsequent time, the experiential learning curve being positive and steep. I took advantage of play areas that kids can enjoy in many airports. These days, in many places, even sensory break rooms are available. Thanks to my husband, we are able to get lounge access when we travel with him, and that is a blessing, too. Noise-cancelling headphones help to reduce the over-stimulating noise. When Rishi was about three or four years old, he had an animal backpack (monkey with a long tail). He loved to walk around and explore, and I could let him do that safely while holding on to the tail. I loved that backpack—and I have been stopped by parents of toddlers across countries, wanting to know where they could purchase one, too.

Just as there were many things to learn about my child, I also had a lot to learn about myself. I think those things are just as pertinent, if not more. Unless we feel everything is under control, the anxiety and stress that we bring can ruin it for everyone around us. We must be able to acknowledge those stressors and work to be in control ourselves. The first lesson I discovered about myself was that I had developed severe motion sickness, especially during long flights. Of course, I learned it the hard way—getting sick and being absolutely miserable in those flights. I needed to feel physically fine and not have to run to the restroom every few minutes. Hence, non-drowsy anti-motion sickness medicines during a long flight are essential for me. Second lesson: Jet lag and the odd food hours during flight make every single passenger uncomfortable. My child is not alone, and

I do not need to feel apologetic toward other passengers—they get it, since they feel it, too. Third, I can try to make as much room as possible in those seats, but they are just uncomfortable. Unless one can afford flying business class, there is no way that children will be in a comfortable space.

A lot has changed for the positive regarding travel over the last twenty years. Earlier, when Rishi was little, we had a laminated travel card stating something like this: "*I am autistic. I may be making noises or moving my body, and this is because this experience is very difficult for me. I am trying my best to deal with it with these actions. Please bear with me.*" Rishi had to hand over this card to his fellow passenger just one time, when he was directly asked to stop moving, making noise and causing disturbance. The passenger at once apologized and complimented him when we disembarked. Other times, good Samaritans have watched the children when I needed a break, or helped my son in the men's toilets if the family restroom was not available at the airport. There have been exceptions as well, when I have been nonchalantly given unsolicited advice from ignorant, loud-mouthed strangers. We received no apologies when they were corrected, just a hasty retreat. But overall, my experiences have been positive, and Rishi has grown to like airplanes a lot.

Again, the key is in the preparation. Some airline carriers have mockups in the airport with a dummy airplane, so special needs families can get used to the flight experience before the real deal. YouTube has videos that can be a great resource to view. It includes videos on airplane interiors, the food served, the general bustle of the airport, and even the white noise in flights. These can be used as part of the preparation and desensitizing process. During the pandemic, when Rishi was clearly missing being on an airplane, he would turn on these videos (which he searched up and discovered independently) for hours on the big screen TV. I was surprised with the "white noise" bit—this used to be a stress factor previously; he always seemed to have a hard time when he was little. Now he misses it and seeks it out.

The real life challenges of air travel are mostly evident in the pre-boarding time. The bustling and busy airport, the long queues, and the security checks with very strict rules and regulations can be very unnerving. In the United States, the Transportation Security Administration (TSA) has a special program called TSA Cares that eases this challenge for individuals with disabilities. All details are available at the TSA website, and so many have benefited from this service. Airlines also provide a pre-board pass at the gate for a sensory-friendly boarding experience. Many of these programs and services have been introduced recently, and they have undergone several changes in the years that we have taken flights. In general, it is always very helpful to call and ask—chances are they may deny, but it is equally likely that adjustment may be made to ease the process. It never hurts to ask.

Fairy Tales and Adventures

The magic of Disney is that world of enchantment that children are enthralled by. Travel to Disney is a very common query in many support groups, hence will share our takeaways from this fun trip. We have been to Orlando four times in a bid to divide and conquer the parks. Just kidding—we need a couple more trips! With the exception of one trip, the others have been during peak holiday season—Thanksgiving and Christmas. The first two trips were when Rishi was 1.5 and 2.5 years old, respectively. We were definitely excited, but we were not entirely sure how much of the Disney experience was actually enjoyable for him. But he positively enjoyed the trip we made in February of 2011—a trip planned especially for his little sister with a heavy dose of princesses thrown in. The little one was star struck with all the royalty as expected, but we were pleasantly surprised to see Rishi absolutely enamored with Sleeping Beauty. He was a little puddle next to Princess Aurora and could not stop staring adoringly at her, and bless her heart, she was indulgent, gentle, and kind in a very regal way. That place is true magic!

At the same time, Disney parks can be very overwhelming for our children. One unique challenge in the parks (other than the l-o-n-g queues) is that it requires considerable effort to get in and out of the parks. After paying a neat little sum for the family's admission tickets, we naturally want to maximize the experience. Accommodation in any of the Disney resorts does have the benefit of multiple entries and use of the internal train as easy transport, thus avoiding the parking lot rigmarole. Services such as disability access service cards and sensory-friendly break rooms are now available in the parks, which would be highly beneficial for our children. When we traveled, these were not yet added—we would use the fast pass system and plan a set of rides and then take a break before the next set. The children's play section, of course, was a high point for our children. It may help to travel in a group—family or friends with similarly aged children—so you could take turns with the rides where the children cannot accompany you.

As part of the preparations or setting expectations process (the antecedent approach as we discussed earlier), it would help to talk to our children and familiarize them with what to expect on the visit. Social stories can be very effective in this regard. As such, they may be implemented in a variety of situations to prime and set expectations of appropriate behaviors, unique events, concepts, social norms, skills, etc. Social stories are written in the first person, and they must directly convey the intended message in short, simple sentences. The language used is descriptive and positive, focusing on what the expectations are and what is to be done. There are many free templates available on the internet, but you can just as easily write one up to customize to your needs. Here is an example of a social story:

SOCIAL STORY ON: TRAVELING TO DISNEY WORLD

On [July 10], we will go on a holiday to Disney World.

We will go in an airplane (or go in our car) for ___ hours and reach Orlando, Florida.

We will go to Magic Kingdom.

We will go on many rides.

We will see Mickey Mouse, Minnie Mouse, Goofy, Pluto, etc.

We will see princesses.

There will be a big castle.

There will be a parade.

It will be noisy. There will be lots of people.

It is okay.

I can ask for a break when I need one.

We will have fun on the trip.

Pictures may be added for a visual reference, and they may even be referenced in the park to connect the learning. In the same manner, social stories can be made for any situation. Something important to keep in mind is that we would use social stories when the child is available to learn. During a challenging behavior episode, the goal is always for the child to regain composure and calm down. Reading out expected behaviors at that moment is akin to "white noise"—your child is too agitated to listen to and process any information, and the social story will be completely ineffective.

Float the Boat

Needless to say, our children work best with consistency and structure, especially in the early stages of learning. We expect these to be in place in a classroom or clinic, and we strive to have a structure at home in the best way possible, but to have a structure during a trip is almost impossible. Other than specific times for traveling in a public transport, it is quite difficult to be consistent and structured. We have discussed quite a lot of strategies in the chapters, such as providing choices, handing responsibilities, and creating social stories for expected events, which may all be used to bring in consistency and structure. Visuals such as a first/then board can be combined with a simple three-step schedule:

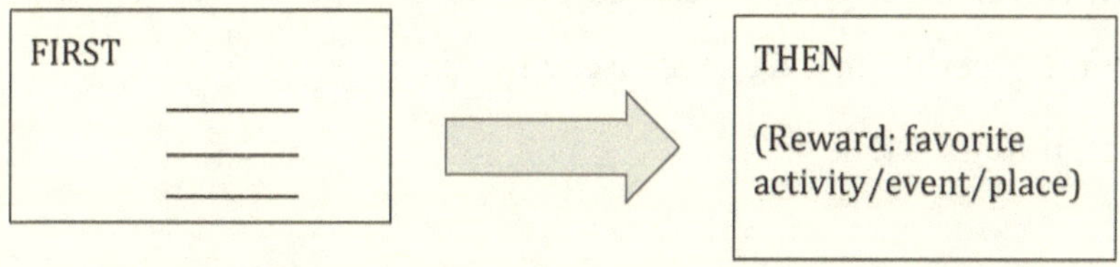

This can be done verbally as well, with the number of activities according to the functioning level of the child.

During travel, with all the novelty and changes that your child has to tolerate and take in stride, it would help to keep the expectations and goals to a level that will be easily attainable by him and your family. There should be little worry for regression—he will pick right back up once he is back to familiar surroundings. Exposure to these expectations by undertaking day trips, weekend trips, and then a longer trip will help shape the behaviors according to your expectations. On a longer trip, a contained space with highly preferred activities (in our case, a beach vacation: a hotel with easy access to the beach and a pool) has little for us to do—but we are able to relax and rejuvenate while Rishi is safe and gleefully content. Graduate to the more activity-filled vacations once the behavioral expectations are in place. And finally, believe! If in your heart there is no inkling of doubt that a particular dream can be achieved, you will move mountains to make that happen. The adage, "Where there is a will, there is a way," holds very true. Even if it is not exactly to the degree you hoped for, there will be an elevation from the prior level, for sure. Optimism and positivity are some of the most powerful tools you possess, so put them to great use. It will all come together one day because, why not?

Bon Voyage!

~~~~~~~~~~~~~~~~
~~~~~~~~~~~~~~~~

AT A GLANCE:

- Plan and prepare with calendars and visuals
- Reinforcing breaks (items/activities) built in
- Making choices and handling responsibilities built in
- Set expectations with to-do lists with a first/then structure
- Social stories help with behavioral expectations

Would you like an adventure now
or shall we have tea first?
—Peter Pan

notes

[1] Source: https://www.nichd.nih.gov/health/topics/autism/conditioninfo/treatments/early-intervention

[2] Source: https://psychcentral.com/pro/child-therapist/2016/12/15-fields-to-apply-applied-behavior-analysis-aba-services#1.

[3] Punishment in behavior analytic terms is not aversive, but any event that decreases the future probability of a behavior. Conceptually, it is the exact opposite of reinforcement, which increases the future probability of a behavior.

[4] A lot of studies can be found in Google Scholar. Institutes such as the Child Mind Institute or the Marcus Autism Center (to name a couple) have practical tips, as do a host of others.

[5] https://pubmed.ncbi.nlm.nih.gov/30880542/

[6] Numerous sleep studies have been conducted. Google Scholar is a good database to search for scholarly articles. Several parent resource websites have collated the updated findings of these studies.

[7] Our choices may have reinforcing and punishing aspects—punishing as understood in behavioral terms. We will stick to reinforcing aspects as the discussion here is on recreation, a reinforcing activity.

[8] Antecedent: What happens before the behavior. Behavior: What the child is demonstrating currently. Consequence: What happens after the behavior.

resources

All ABA concepts mentioned in this book are from: J.O. Cooper, T.E. Heron, W.L. Howard, *Applied Behavior Analysis*, Second Edition (2007).

Each of these chapters can be a book by itself, but Google Scholar is an excellent place to search for peer reviewed published articles on ABA.

There are many websites that offer information on the topics visited here. Information may be accessed in the Health and Human Resources websites, many parent support organization websites, and therapy provider web pages.

Pivotal Response Training: Koegel Autism Center, https://education.ucsb.edu/autism

Verbal Behavior: Cambridge Center for Behavioral Studies, https://behavior.org/

Early Start Denver Model: https://www.esdm.co/

Floortime: https://www.icdl.com/floortime

Relationship Development Intervention: https://www.rdiconnect.com/about-rdi/

www.ingramcontent.com/pod-product-compliance
Lightning Source LLC
LaVergne TN
LVHW090943080826
845145LV00003B/876

* 9 7 8 1 9 5 6 2 6 7 1 0 5 *